Laura's New Heart

A Healer's Spiritual Journey Through a Heart Transplant

by Laura L. Fine

ISBN: 1-4140-6434-9 (e-book)
ISBN: 1-4140-6433-0 (Paperback)

This book is printed on acid free paper.

Distributed by
A Quantum Reach Publishing
a-quantum-reach.com
Edited by Ruth Mullen · Cover Design byGail Jorden
Layout by Jerri-Jo Idarius

1stBooks – rev. 02/03/04

Acknowledgements

Who do I thank for a new heart? First and foremost, I thank my Divine Beloved for this opportunity to have another day to think of Him; my Spiritual Master for giving me *His* heart and S.D.,—your words of wisdom and guidance mean more to me than you know; my sister for going above and beyond the call of duty; Dara for her words of encouragement; Steve for letting me know you're in my corner; Kenny and Anita, you never stop being there for me—I have no words; cousin Sue and the Fine clan, you make me proud to bear our name; Jessica and Judy, no time ever passes from last life to this one. Next time we share together, let's just try to find a different excuse for the rendezvous. Beth, Mary, Kathy, Mina, nothing is as nurturing as home-cooked meals delivered with hugs. I wish to honor the countless doctors, nurses and healers who helped save my body, my mind and my emotional heart, the healing touch nurses, Judson and the energy healers. Dr. Jaski, you are more than just a world series player in medicine. Thank you for adding the magic of genuine love and caring to your ministry. Joan and Judy, how can I express my gratitude for your unending patience, grace, expertise and integrity? I am truly trying my best not to take advantage! A special honor to you, Dr. Mimi Guarneri. You never gave up on me. Without your crucial timing, decisions and recognition of who I am, I wouldn't be here today. Rauni, my healer, my friend, my fellow crusader, my teacher, thank you. Rob, your emotional support, love and encouragement, your way of seeing me has helped me to integrate my experience back into the land of the living. And finally I wish to honor my donor for willing me the inheritance of your beautiful heart and your family for its delivery to my doorstep.

If I had to summarize the most precious spiritual understanding I have received from this experience, I could say this: "God has given me the opportunity to experience a depth of gratitude I had never touched. Gratitude has enabled me to experience more love."

Thank you

Laura

Table of Contents

Acknowledgments   3

Introduction   7

Chapter One: The Quest   9

Chapter Two: Always Beeping   23

Chapter Three: Sodi Water   45

Chapter Four: Denial   64

Chapter Five: I'm Alive, It's a Good Day   80

Chapter Six: Laura's New Heart   113

Chapter Seven: Assimilation   129

Appendix I   Affirmations   137

Appendix I   Organ Donation   141

End Notes   145

Introduction

On January 18, 2001, I had a heart transplant. Writing my story was something I felt compelled to do. The cathartic process of writing has helped me to digest and integrate my survival of a traumatic near-death experience. Today my health and quality of life is normal. It's almost as if the entire experience is like a blip on the screen of memory. I now re-read my own words and work to remember the level of transcendent realizations, gratitude and humility that spontaneously occurred throughout this journey. This has become a part of my spiritual practice, one that I am happy to embrace.

We live in a culture segregated from death and dying. This separation results in an unfortunate spiritual price for us all. My experiences have gifted me with priceless understandings, some of which I do my best to convey to you. Like many trauma survivors there is a desire to remember, to relive, a longing to understand and embody the deep spiritual mysteries that are awakened when we walk alongside the reality of our mortality.

As you journey with me, I encourage you to journey with yourself, reflecting on your own mortality. As you read the story I encourage you to slow down and take the time to speak aloud the affirmations that are interspersed among the text. I repeated them in my mind hundreds of time to ease my mental stress through challenging moments. You may wish to utilize the open-ended sentences at the end of each chapter to inspire your own internal exploration and self-discovery. The thought invitations are designed to take you into the subconscious layers of your mind where they will stimulate your imagination, creativity and inspire your self-reflective insights.

Also in reading this book, know that it is in no way intended as a prostelization of my particular spiritual practice. I believe each person's spiritual beliefs and relationship are personal, sacred and unique to that individual. Please take what you like.

I send you wishes to become increasingly aware of God's blessings and love constantly showering upon you with each beat of your heart.

Chapter One: *The Quest*

I had never had a heart transplant before. That was a first.

I was healthy all my life and worked as a holistic health practitioner. Then I got heart failure. No one knows why. Seems ironic. My life is different now. I have come to regard this experience as part of my destiny and am awed, humbled and extremely grateful for what has happened to me. Just as this body is on loan for this lifetime, I have been given another loan—a new heart to sustain this body for some unknown length of time, in order to continue to deepen my spiritual growth. How incredibly blessed I am. This has also been the most challenging, difficult and magnificent time of my life. The extremes of this experience of miracles and helplessness, the synchronicity of God's Divine mercy and compassion are beyond expression.

Let's back up to some other firsts in my life. My conscious spiritual search first began unconsciously when I was twenty-one years old. I noticed a friend of mine, who had been deeply troubled, becoming very happy. I asked her what happened.

"I started going to therapy," Carol proclaimed.

"Therapy? What on earth for?"

"I just want to work on my relationship with Ron."

They seemed to be a happy and well-suited couple. Why on earth was she going for therapy? I was intrigued by the idea. It was clear that Carol was different, happier. I wasn't particularly unhappy, but my curiosity was aroused.

I pondered on a reason to go for therapy. My life was moving along nicely. I had recently moved to Miami Florida with my husband. We were living together in a tiny apartment. I had gotten my first professional work in the theatre as an equity stage manager with Coconut Grove Playhouse, teaching movement for actors at Florida International University and was being paid to direct community theatre. Life was good. My immediate career leap from College into the professional world happened more easily than I could have imagined, but I wasn't bubblingly happy like Carol. What was it? What reason could I give to a therapist for making an appointment? I enjoyed sex with my husband and experienced orgasm and gratification but it never sounded quite as exciting as how my friend Anne described her sexual relationship with her husband. I figured I hadn't achieved the potential pleasure that sex could offer so I figured that was a worthy psychological excuse to get started in therapy. I was amazed at the results that occurred in just a few brief sessions of hypnotherapy. I was in awe of the power that began to come out of my body and dazzled by this teacher who seemed to know just how to tap into that part of me. I wanted to know all the secrets, my own secrets that I was not yet aware of, and her secrets. How did she manage to have such a profound impact on me? I discovered that the therapist also led a meditation group. I was fascinated.

When I walked into her home for my first meditation experience I entered a part of the house I had not really seen before. It was separated from the room where we had our therapy treatments. I was uncomfortable and apprehensive. There were pictures of Christ everywhere, painted on the walls, decorating the tables. Being Jewish born to a nonreligious family that grew up in a Catholic neighborhood, one concept had been drilled deeply into me that began as a very young girl. "Jesus Christ is NOT your savior! When everyone says the Lord's Prayer at school, you don't have to say it. Just stand and fold your hands, but you don't have to say it. We're Jews. We don't believe in Jesus Christ." I never understood why I didn't believe in him or who he was, or what he did that I shouldn't believe in him. But it was clearly repeated that he was "just a man, not God. He was a great teacher, but he is not your savior."

These thoughts flashed immediately through my head as I entered the darkened candlelit room with incense burning and an air of anticipation. What was I doing here? I'm a Jewish girl. I don't belong here. But there was a feeling in the room that was spiritually exciting, something I had never felt before in any church or Synagogue. It drew me in. The talk and the meditation touched a deep chord of longing in my being. I felt love for God. That was a surprise. How could that be? At that time in my life I wasn't even sure if I believed in God! My mind was stirred and confused. My husband didn't approve. Also Jewish born and bred he was sure I had stumbled into a cult. I could not resist going. My heart was too hungry for spiritual truth and knowledge. I felt a 'high' that no drug or alcohol could touch. It was such a gratifying feeling that I quit smoking cigarettes and drinking and any occasional use of recreational drugs.

That experience marked the beginning of a conscious spiritual search. I meditated twice daily without fail. In the satsang talks I learned an esoteric and eastern perspective of Christ. I had my first experience of spiritual love. I fell in love with Christ. I began to have an inkling of what all the fuss was about him. I was delighted. I started putting up pictures of Christ all over my home. My husband could not tolerate these drastic changes in me. We were both so very young and ill equipped to emotionally deal with our differences. A short time later we were divorced.

I threw myself into my spiritual practice. I spent three years devoutly committed to my meditation practice, an hour in the morning, an hour in the evening. The search took me in a multitude of directions. I became a vegetarian. I prided myself on my natural lifestyle and spiritual seeking. A new world opened up. I had been a theatre major and dance minor in college. Always drawn to physical development I began years of disciplined exercise in yoga, tai chi, and creative movement. I jogged five miles a day without fail. I ate a pure raw food vegetarian diet. I slept no more than five hours a night as my energy level was exponentially intensified by my disciplined regimen. I felt like I was walking six feet off the ground. I started massage school and polarity energy training. I felt like a reformed smoker. I wanted to run away from everything that seemed to contain impurity, selfishness and vanity. I wanted to quit theatre as I didn't understand how to reconcile that lifestyle and morality with my new found spiritual practice. I felt torn but committed. After reaching the 'highest level' of initiation I could achieve with this meditation teacher, I moved into the inner circle of those closest to her.

At that time, I started to observe disconcerting behaviors in this teacher and therapist I had so idolized. I saw her imperfections, the subtle ways she was selfish, greedy, self-centered and using her sexuality inappropriately. What was going on?! How could this be? It was hugely devastating. I was disappointed and deeply saddened. Now what? Now how would I grow spiritually? I drifted away from the group, from the spiritual community that had cost me my marriage and had been the central focus of my life for three years.

I missed the theatre. I had had enough of this self-imposed abstinence based upon misguided instructions of a self-proclaimed spiritual teacher who had herself been a former actress. As I explored other spiritual directions I began to learn that people in spiritual organizations (like in all other businesses), were full of ego and human imperfection. I held onto my belief and love for God and my meditation practice. I would make my own relationship with my Beloved God. I began to read books and found solace in the writings of esoteric and spiritual teachers such as Rudolf Steiner, Alice Bailey and Hilda Charlton. I was also drawn to east Indian philosophies.

I then decided to go back to teaching and acting. I missed the theater and wanted to find a way to incorporate my newly discovered spiritual principles into my work as a director and acting teacher.

I had known from an early age that I was a natural born teacher. I have a distinct memory of arriving in first grade and already knowing how to read. I don't know how I knew. No one ever taught me. I remember sitting at my little desk, incredibly bored as the children were laboring over, "Run, Spot, run, run, run." It all seemed so stupid to my five-year-old mind and I was irritated at the teacher. Even the children who were struggling to learn were bored. I distinctly remember thinking, "It's the teacher's responsibility to make this fun for us. She isn't doing that!" Perhaps that was the day that my teaching destiny was determined.

Standing in front of a classroom is comfortable and exhilarating for me. If I understand something, I can teach it. In front of any group of students, I forget myself and become immersed in the needs of the audience. I thrive on the challenge to make learning fun, to be available and present.

Still in my twenties, I never had a problem getting professional work, so after deciding to teach acting once again, it wasn't long before I was on the theatre staff with three different colleges. I felt uplifted. Teaching was a respite. I trained hundreds of actors and in between jobs I worked as a massage therapist—incorporating energy healing into the massage and into my teaching as well.

Relationships were not so easy. My divorce had been followed by yet another disappointing relationship and I knew I had to make a drastic change. On a visit home to my mother in Cincinnati I interviewed at the Cincinnati Playhouse and got a job setting up an acting training program for children and adults and a position as a directing intern with the Intern Company. I was thirty-one. This felt like a good career move and a pit stop toward my eventual goal of moving to New York City. I had reconciled that I could still be 'spiritual' and pursue my passion for theatre. I began to land professional directing jobs in regional theatre and almost always managed to receive good reviews. Perhaps I didn't have to let go of my dream to conquer Broadway, to become artistic director of my own theatre company, settle in to a nurturing relationship and perhaps have a family. Three years of hard work built up a successful acting training program for the professional theatre company only to be followed by budget cuts, managerial changes at the theatre, and the end of another romance. It was clearly time for the big leap.

After moving to New York City, my career rapidly blossomed. I affiliated myself with several prestigious theatre companies and also continued to travel and direct professional regional theatre. After four years building an acting training program with Riverside Shakespeare Company in New York City, I landed my first Off-Broadway show.

In the midst of a dreadful rehearsal process, I took a break to trade massages with a colleague. When we finished, he pulled out a book on energy healing. It depicted pictures of auras, chakras and energy fields. One look at the vividly vibrant pictures was all I needed to recognize these were depictions of sensations and experiences that both my clients and myself had been describing during their treatments. I exclaimed, "I've been looking for this understanding for years." Soon after, I began formal schooling in energy healing.

Along with attending rehearsals in the high pressured theatrical arena, I began an intensive four-year training program in energy healing. This changed my life. Working on myself helped me understand aspects of my personality and habitual defense mechanisms and this became more important to me than the theatre. It took my heart out of the "show." The rehearsal process suffered and the artistic director was less than pleased and although I felt overwhelmed, we managed to get through it. The show was a great success and was extended three months. Yet, I was disillusioned. The 'magic' and creative joy in directing Off-Broadway was frozen—devoured by the pressures and financial fears of the producers and backers. The stress of working under conditions where lots of money and investments were at stake was more than I felt emotionally equipped to handle, and the 'thrill' and aspiration of making it to Broadway faded.

After fifteen years in theater, I felt ready to walk away. Though the creative process was delightful, I did not enjoy the emotional upheaval of leaving home and friends to work with strangers with whom I would quickly bond but never see again. I chose instead to stay focused on my teaching career and immediately integrated what I was learning about the chakra and energy system into training professional actors. In the midst of performing, my students began having profound emotional releases accompanied by deep personal insights. Their performances were electrifying. Spontaneous healing was a frequent side effect. I left many acting classes muttering, "I'm not teaching acting, I'm teaching healing. Am I cheating my students?"

In the meantime I continued my spiritual seeking. This quest took me deeper into the study of psychic healing and all the modalities that were in vogue—Polarity Therapy®, Feldenkrais®, Alexander Technique®, reflexology, massage, energy healing. I studied with famous healers and instructors and now developed a dual career which combined the creative and healing arts. I ran from one training program to the next while developing a strong base of students and clients. I utilized theatre games, improv and creativity exercises to relax self-consciousness, open energy blockages, and help students to intimately communicate and connect with their clients. Students created spontaneous and healing poetry, sounds, songs, dance and movement patterns to affect their own energy fields and those of their clients. I left these classes shaking my head thinking, "I'm not teaching healing, I'm teaching acting. Am I cheating my healers?" I learned that…

Healing is creating and creating is healing.

> ("Is this really what they signed up for?" It's getting so emotional in the classroom!")

Healing is creating and creating is healing.

> ("It's okay—what happened in the classroom today. John really came into his power, he was crying and laughing at the same time.")

Healing is creating and creating is healing.

> ("My God, I've never seen such spontaneity in Bob before…I must be doing something right.")

This statement really was true. I had always felt magical moments of alchemical transformation when I taught but now something different was happening in the classroom—something even more unexplainable. The results were intimately related to the subtle energy system of human physiology. My doubts receded over time. The actors consistently performed magnificently. The healers had a powerful effect on their clients. Everyone was having fun! Healing is creating and creating is healing. It mattered little from which direction we came. The results were rapid, creative, transformational and fun!

My priorities were shifting. Experiences with subtle energy whet my appetite for greater spiritual truth and knowledge. I spent the next two years studying Kabbalistic healing and meditation with one spiritual teacher and healer after another. Next I was exposed to the ancient

Vedic scriptures and was spellbound hearing their profound yet simple truths. My teacher gave common sense teachings about life's deepest mysteries. "Why I was born?" "What is my purpose?" These questions resonated deep within me. When he offered me an opportunity to move to the West Coast to help start a healing school, I didn't hesitate for a moment. I was happy to leave New York City for a more peaceful and healthy environment in San Diego, near the Pacific Ocean. I took this opportunity to grow as a teacher and manage a successful healing training program at the peak of the 'New Age' movement.

Co-creating a healing school enabled me to integrate all my previous skills. All my former experiences had simply prepared me for this, what I thought to be my true calling. The program achieved rapid success, but over time, this experience also dulled. As with former teachers, inevitably I witnessed their human flaws—the same as were in me—greed, lust and selfishness. I plodded along outwardly happy to be helping the students yet inwardly frustrated and disappointed. In each setting, it seemed impossible for all concerned to purely practice what we were preaching. I felt like a hypocrite and was caught in a paradox. We were helping, but helpless. Why were gifted teachers incapable of acknowledging their human weaknesses? Had we all become masters of subtle pretension—hiding even from ourselves? I was sick with disillusionment.

One day I took a walk along Pacific Beach. Tears were streaming down my face. I was facing the disillusion of yet another illusion of perfection. I prayed inwardly to God, "I know that it's You I really want, dear Lord. If I just find You, I know I would be happy. I know that it is not these other things that bring happiness. I know it is You that I want." I felt numb. I walked through my life desensitized, feeling empty, abandoned by everyone and everything. Now what? I had tried everything. There were no real teachers left.

LAURA'S NEW HEART — The Quest

Then a turning point occurred. I was introduced to a rasik Saint from India who taught a spiritual practice based in Vedic Scriptures. He taught with a purity and Grace I had never known. My skepticism was so strengthened by past disappointments that it took many months before I felt safe enough to begin to surrender to the truth I was hearing. Twenty years of conscious spiritual seeking filled with distorted 'New Age' concepts were finally being corrected and dispelled through his teachings. My perspective opened and clarified. What impressed me immediately was the way in which he distinguished psychic-healing from true spiritual devotion and love for God. He clarified and explained subtle distinctions and truths that I had been unable to articulate. Over time as truth was clarified, my fears of repeated disappointment relaxed and my heart soared with new feelings of love for God.

I was also in a comfortable relationship with a man. All was well. Though the relationship was short lived it no longer mattered. I had finally found a true path to God. I knew that all would be well. I was growing spiritually. Detachment from the relationship occurred without so much pain because I was spiritually happier than I had ever been. I devoured all fourteen of my teacher's books and incorporated the practice of Bhakti Yog, a path of intimate personal relationship with God into my life. I could find no flaw in this Divinely realized teacher. I finally began a real spiritual practice. It took time.

Laura Fine with Students · 1995
Teaching the energy System of Acting

LAURA'S NEW HEART — The Quest

My eyes drift inward on a deep search for my soul buried within my heart center. The pull of worldly attractions tease my mind but I linger longer there in the quiet of my heart till I notice the breeze like stirring of my soul's cry...

_____

_____

_____

_____

_____

_____

_____

_____

_____

_____

_____

_____

_____

_____

The images above are an invitation to self-reflect, explore and discover more of the depths of your soul's mysterious beauty. You may wish to utilize the space above to respond to the image, designed to stimulate your creative subconscious mind. Taking a few minutes to journal your response to the thought, invites an opportunity to deepen your contact with your loving spiritual nature.

It whispers sweetly on my tongue singing it's cry of longing that says…

Chapter Two: *Always Beeping*

In January of 2000 I reassessed my life. I seldom got sick but whenever I did, I applied foot-reflexology, saw a chiropractor, did a dietary fast and colon cleanse. I can count on one hand the times I resorted to taking an aspirin. I maintained good health and struggled only with allergies. No matter how many dietary restrictions or alternative treatments I imposed, I could not seem to get them in check.

Now in my mid-forties my career was doing well. My life was calm and peaceful. I was not in a relationship, but for the first time I felt full and fulfilled without one. Yet, I was tired and sometimes found myself quickly short of breath when I tried to exercise or walk briskly. I simply figured I was out of shape and needed more discipline.

While on a plane to San Antonio to teach a workshop in Transpersonal Energy Healing, I realized I wasn't able to walk from one airport terminal to the next to make my connection. I needed a wheelchair. As I was pushed along by the porter, I chuckled at myself, thinking, "Something is wrong with this picture." I thought it was asthma as I had been having trouble breathing, but I didn't know you could feel so tired and nauseous from asthma. Something didn't add up. More than asthma was wrong with me. I called my friend Steve, an M.D. from Cincinnati, and he told me, "Get a chest x-ray."

"You must be kidding," I said, "It's really not that bad." Why would I want to expose myself to an unnecessary zap of toxic radiation?

As my symptoms refused to go away, I finally made an appointment with my doctor. She assumed it was asthma too and prescribed an inhaler. This gave me a brief respite and I was sure I could go about the business of wholistically investigating and treating asthma. I resisted using the inhaler for fear of the toxic affect of the steroid in my lungs. When the shortness of breath refused to go away and I did give in to using the inhaler, it took only two weeks to realize that the drug was not alleviating my symptoms at all. My doctor wanted me to get a chest x-ray to be sure it was asthma. I refused. Being an HHP, I was going to cure my asthma with acupuncture, diet, essential oils and energy healing—*certainly* not worsen my condition by exposing myself to the unnecessary radiation of a chest x-ray! When Bunny, my friend and sponsor of the workshop I was going to teach, picked me up at the San Antonio airport, I informed her that I was not at all feeling well. I was extremely fatigued, was having trouble breathing, was a bit nauseated and very concerned that I would not have the strength to teach. I asked Bunny to take me to her naturopathic chiropractor. She had often sung praises of his expertise and sensitivity. He told me to go and get a chest x-ray. Finally, after hearing this advice from three different medical professionals, I paid attention.

Bunny took me to the Urgent Care center. The doctor who examined me posted the x-ray in front of the light box. She looked at me in shock.

"How are you even walking? You have a lake of fluid in your lungs and your heart is enlarged. I'm sending you immediately to a cardiologist."

The cardiologist put me through an extensive series of tests – EKG, stress, and echocardiogram. The nurse checked my vital signs and my weight.

"How much do I weigh?" I hadn't been on a scale for a long time and my pants were fitting a bit tighter so I was curious. I thought I might have gained two or three pounds.

"One hundred eighteen," she reported.

I laughed out loud. "I've never weighed a hundred eighteen in my life!" I'd always been skinny. In fact, it was an effort for me to gain weight. My normal weight usually ranged from one hundred six to one hundred eight pounds.

"I think you should check your scale," I said, concerned. "It really must be off."

The nurse threw me a dirty look and left. I was sincerely trying to help. I was in a joyful mood. I was getting ready to teach a class. I felt ill, but unworried.

The cardiologist sat me down and with a very serious expression announced, "Ms. Fine, you have congestive heart failure (chf).

I repeated his words in my mind, "heart failure." Well, that didn't sound so bad. I mean, it's not cancer, how bad can it be. It was actually kind of comforting to know there was a name for what I had been feeling.

"Your heart is pumping with an ejection fraction (ef) of 25%."

"What does that mean?"

"A normal heart pumps 55-60% of blood through the body with each beat. Yours is functioning at about 25%."

"Well, no big deal, I could heal that!" I thought. I didn't say it out loud. After all he was looking far too grim and I didn't want to spoil his mood. Being a pride-filled holistic health practitioner (HHP) and teacher of energetic hands-on healing, I was self-aware and in control of all my body processes, or so I thought.

"Well, what about Co-Q10 and all those supplements for the heart? Should I start on that? Are there dietary changes I should make?"

"There's really no research to back up their effectiveness." Obviously he had not much knowledge or belief in alternative healing!

"What caused it?"

"There's no way of telling. Perhaps a virus, we don't know. Just watch your salt intake."

The doctor immediately started me on a pulse of diuretics to drain my lungs, prescribed a low dose beta-blocker, and told me to find a cardiologist when I got back to San Diego. He sent me on my way. Draining my lungs with diuretics brought immediate relief. With the help of my two teaching assistants, I taught the workshop and had a wonderful time.

When I returned home to San Diego, I got on the web and began to research chf. I learned that an ef of under 30% qualified you for a heart transplant. Heart transplant! You've got to be kidding. They obviously never tried acupuncture or alternative healing.

At the same time, I began my search for a cardiologist. That was another first—needing a *cardiologist* at forty-five years of age? I had initial consultations with two different doctors who had never heard of the words "holistic health practitioner." One gave me a gloom-and-doom report assuring me that I would certainly get worse, wanted to start me immediately on a litany of drugs and return in two weeks for an evaluation for a pacemaker. What on earth was he talking about? Was he a quack? I was furious at his cold insensitivity.

He wrote prescriptions for a long list of drugs with even longer names that you couldn't pronounce. Each drug had a list of appalling side affects. He handed me the list of drugs like he was handing me a death warrant and with a cold and serious face apologized for giving me such grim news. He emphatically instructed me to return in two weeks, check into a hospital and be evaluated for a pacemaker. Are you kidding! I thought he was incredibly brazen. Are doctors really as stupid as I'd been hearing all these years? Hand me a death warrant list of drugs with almost no explanation and command me to come back in two weeks to be cut open. Most amazing of all was that he actually expected I would do it! Was he an idiot?

When I left his office I exhaled a deep sigh of relief telling myself this was his narrow minded negative perspective, all the while using a mantra to stave off the subtle fear creeping its way into my subconscious mind.

I inhale discernment, I exhale judgment.

("What an ass, does he think he is God!")

I inhale discernment, I exhale judgment.

("Okay, don't think like that, it's okay. Yikes! How can I possibly do what he says?")

I inhale discernment, I exhale judgment.

("Oh my God. Of course! I'll simply get a second opinion, make another plan.")

I knew I would never step foot in his office again. After hours surfing the net and phone calls all over the country, I wormed my way into the network of doctors and cardiologists who were educated in wholistic health and open to alternative and complimentary medicine. Combining cardiology and complimentary medicine was such a rare and specialized mix. I kept looking and calling. They were scattered around other parts of the country. I tried to continue seeing clients, but I wasn't feeling well. Time was of the essence. I needed to get started with someone I could communicate with at least a little. I tried several other highly recommended western doctors. They were compassionate and knowledgeable but had no clue of the meaning of energy healing. How would I bridge this gap? Through a circuitous route via my friend Steve in Cincinnati, I learned of Dr. Erminia Guarneri, a highly reputable cardiologist who is the director of Scripps Center for Integrative Medicine. Scripps offers alternative healing modalities—healing touch, stress management, yoga, nutritional counseling, group counseling and meditation. I felt a thrill go through my body. Dr. Guarneri was for me.

When I called her office, her secretary curtly informed me that she already had 1500 patients and was not taking any new cases. "Oh my God, now what?" I was dismayed. Now what would I do? Who else could I turn to in San Diego? I had to find a way in. I knew that if she met me, I would have a shot at convincing her to take my case. I tried calling her at the Integrative Medicine Center where I got the receptionist Tina on the line. I pleaded my case to Tina, told her of my background, told her my story and that I had never been sick a day in my life. Tina was moved. She agreed to help me try to get in contact with Dr. Guarneri and suggested I write a letter. I told Tina, "I'll fax it to you in an hour. Just promise me you will hand deliver it to the doctor yourself." She promised. I composed the letter, exhaled and surrendered. I thought I'd give it a few weeks, keep looking and turn my attention elsewhere. Two days later, Dr. Guarneri called me herself and invited me to come in for an appointment. I sobbed with relief. Our first meeting surpassed my expectations. Not only did she know about hands-on energy healing, she'd been trained in it herself. She spent close to an hour with me in our first consultation and exam. She did not seem in a hurry. How could that be? I slowed down my frantic pace of questions and began to relax. She was taking her time, it gave me permission to do the same. Her loving compassion and pragmatic brilliance were hope for real healing.

She wanted to start me on two carefully selected heart medications. I immediately resisted the idea and had to be convinced of the effectiveness, value and sense of each pill. After all, I had hardly taken an aspirin all my life! Okay, two, I could handle two. It was better than the six meds that the gloom and doom doc wanted me to start on. I couldn't understand why she hadn't yet figured out a regimen of natural remedies, but I trusted her enough to accept her protocol. It was enough of a stretch to understand that she truly did believe in and understand western medicine as well as alternative healing. I had to open my mind. She kept a close watch on me and scheduled regular monthly visits. I was concerned about the side affects of the medications. I had kept my body chemistry relatively pure through diet, fasting and cleansing for over twenty-five years. I did not want to distort my system with drugs. I didn't *feel* sick. Picking up prescription drugs stirred challenges to my biases. I gazed at the pill bottles. This is old lady stuff. Why was this happening? These drugs will only alleviate some of my symptoms, perhaps take some of the stress off my heart but they won't heal me; they won't cure the illness. I was still left with the dilemma of how I was going to *really heal?*

I was tired all the time. Being a type A personality, feeling tired all the time was a first too. Well, actually, I got tired in the afternoons, shortly after lunch. I thought, "Maybe I have chronic fatigue syndrome." I began to have more empathy for that illness. I didn't put it together that this fatigue was a symptom of heart failure. Other than being tired and sometimes short of breath it was hard to realize that anything was really *wrong* with me. It wasn't as though I had a fever, or a cold, flu, aches or pains somewhere or couldn't function. Chf is a mysterious illness. It was difficult to pinpoint and identify what it was to have chf. I kept thinking I was getting lazy, or that I was out of shape and needed to exercise more frequently.

I had no basis or framework to recognize this illness. Whenever I got a headache or didn't feel well I would do reflexology and yoga. If I got a cold or flu I would take herbs and be well in a matter of days. Dr. Guarneri understood my perspective and we worked minimally (sometimes to her chagrin) with the medications. I took 100 mg. tablets of Co-Q10 and other supplements for the heart. I continued to educate myself, but I didn't know what books to read. All the books I came across were about cardiovascular disease. That was not what I had. My diet and exercise had been excellent. What happened? No one had an explanation. I asked hundreds of questions of every doctor and nurse with whom I came in contact. I learned what each medication did and its side effects. Chf was not going to stop my life. I began acupuncture, took supplements, went through an extensive metabolic testing and typing program to change my diet, got energy healings, went to therapy, did all the things a trained HHP would naturally do.

One morning in April of 2000 I awoke feeling more energy in my body. I called my friend Mina to join me for a walk along the beach. We walked at a good pace for about twenty-five minutes, more than I had achieved in quite some time! I felt happy, perhaps the acupuncture was working and my heart condition was improving! I sat down briefly to rest when suddenly my left leg seized up in indescribable pain. This couldn't be a leg cramp, did something strange happen because of my medications? I had no idea. I could not walk. I started utilizing a rapid breath of fire kundalini breathing technique and a mental affirmation to calm myself and to help me remain mobile.

I breathe in God's love, I breathe out fear.

("I'm okay; You're okay, Laura, Don't worry; It's just you're leg. Everything is okay.")

I breathe in God's love, I breathe out fear.

("Ohhhhh, it really hurts. I'm okay, I'm okay. I'm okay.")

I breathe in God's love, I breathe out fear.

("I can get through this, I'll make it, just hang on. I'm okay. I'm okay. I'm okay.")

I had never in my life felt this kind of excruciating pain. It was 8 a.m. at the beach on a Thursday morning. We had no money with us, but somehow had to find a cab. This wasn't New York City. Where were we going to find a cab? Mina dashed off and fifty feet away out of nowhere appeared a cab! A wonder. While he drove us home I massaged my leg and worked the pressure points. I used a short panting yoga breath to keep from screaming out the pain. Once home, we paid him. Mina helped me up the stairs and I phoned Dr. Guarneri. When I couldn't reach her, I called my M.D. She instructed me to go to the hospital immediately. Meanwhile, the massage seemed to help and the pain level began to decrease slightly. Mina shuttled me into her car and drove me to the hospital. We waited some three-and-a-half hours in Urgent Care. My frustration was mounting. The pain had progressively decreased so I turned to Mina and said, "Let's go home." Just then my name was called to proceed to the examining room.

The doctor examined me, took an ekg, blood pressure, and felt my neck, leg and ankle pulses. The ankle pulse was weak. He seemed to think there might be arterial blockage. He looked up my record on the computer and read over my history of heart failure. Apparently, I had had a blood clot. It was probably caused by a stagnant pool of blood that had gathered around the heart due to the weakness of its pumping ability. My sudden outburst of energy on my walk with Mina worked my heart harder than it had worked for several weeks, and the clot got pumped through my body by the sudden exertion of walking. If it had traveled into the brain instead of the leg, it would have killed me. The clot must have broken off about a half-hour after the pain first hit, which was why the pain was suddenly alleviated.

It was now about 9 p.m. Thursday evening. I was sent for a leg scan. The vascular doctor said there was still arterial blockage.

"I want to check you into the hospital right away and begin an intravenous anticoagulant."

At least he asked my permission instead of informing me.

"Why do I have to do it in the hospital? Aren't you going to just give me a shot?"

"We have to administer the anticoagulant intravenously. The IV drip will probably take a long time. With your heart condition, you really need to be monitored and examined by the cardiologist and vascular doctor."

"Okay." What could I say? It seemed to make sense. I knew my heart was weak. A nurse showed up to insert a catheter in my wrist.

"You want to shove that huge thing into my vein?" I had never had anything like that before. I was squeamish even about receiving a shot. In the next moment she is shoving oxygen tubing up my nose.

"Just hold on a minute, slow down will you! What is the purpose of that?"

"This is standard procedure."

"What are you talking about? I am not standard procedure. Why do I need to be on oxygen? I'm breathing just fine! What is the purpose of this? Did the doctor order it?"

"No, we just do this for all heart problems."

"I'd like to talk to the doctor about it first."

"I will let him know. Meantime, you'll have to put this on."

"No, I don't *have* to do anything."

"There are no contraindications for using oxygen."

"I'm not incapacitated here, I'd like to put it on myself." She kept trying to shove the tubing up my nose.

"Alright fine."

"It's too strong. I can't take it. Can you adjust the flow to make it less intense?"

"Yes, alright." She was peeved. I had slowed her pace. It was as though she resented my questions. I explained to her this was all new to me. Didn't she get that? I was the patient, not her. Why was she mad at me? I was the one on the receiving end of this horrible news. I was the one who had just been committed to the hospital, not her. I was the one who was afraid, though it seemed neither of us could recognize that my defensive attitude and attempts at control were expressions of that fear.

So began my first hospital stay. Being in the hospital was always something that happened to someone else, not to me. It was shocking to be there. As they wheeled me from the emergency room along the corridor toward my room on the cardiac wing, I peered into the open doors I passed. Most people looked elderly. That was somehow oddly reassuring. Obviously I didn't belong here, but things were happening too fast for me to feel afraid. I was in survival mode.

Having heard innumerable horror stories about accidental deaths, wrong drugs administered, etc., I was hyper-vigilant. I was amazed that no one offered explanations about what would happen—that there would be lab techs coming in to draw blood, nurses doing frequent vital sign checks, x-rays, catheters, weight checks, details I couldn't have possibly imagined or expected. Everyone seemed to be on automatic pilot and in a hurry. I felt completely out of control and invisible. Then I got scared. So I began with questions: What is this drug for? Who ordered it? Why? What will it do? What are the side effects? What happens if I don't take it? Why do you want to put me on oxygen when I'm breathing just fine? Why do you need to put in a catheter, why can't you just give me a shot? I don't want that thing hanging out of my arm. They just took my blood pressure downstairs five minutes ago; do you really need to do it again? Can't you just look on the chart? I wouldn't let the nurses or the lab staffs draw my blood or touch me if they were in a hurry or in an agitated state, and many of them were in a hurry or in an agitated state. I was put through another battery of tests and treated with a slow IV drip of anticoagulant. I was told I would be on the IV drip for two days. "Two days! Why so long?" I thought I'd be going home in the morning. After some internal wrestling, I resigned myself to being there and decided to regard the time as an intriguing adventure.

Just for today, I choose to accept, an unacceptable situation.

> "There must be a reason for this. I don't know what it is, but there must be a reason.")

Just for today, I choose to accept, an unacceptable situation.

> *("Okay, you're here now, just relax, unplanned time off. I'll just have Mina bring my book and cancel my appointments.")*

Just for today, I choose to accept, an unacceptable situation.

> ("Well, I don't have to worry about cooking tomorrow, that's good.")

Anyone who knows hospitals knows the constancy of inconstant beeping. Everything beeps, all the time, without musical interval. The IV drips beep, the ekg machines beep, the telemonitors beep. Beeps come intermittently from every direction. Nurses dash from beep to beep trying to get them under control.

I thought about how I would use all these events in my teaching in the classroom, but somehow those thoughts did not console my fears, the stress or discomfort I was in. In my mind I had to effort to stay open and receptive. Then I made a startling realization. I was so busy teaching others in my own mind, that I was missing the lessons myself. I was so busy attempting to deflect my own pain and fear that I kept taking myself out of the moment. Oh my God, I thought…

Don't teach Laura, learn.

> ("How sneakily arrogant I am. I am the one who needs to learn, to be humbled here, not anyone else.")

Don't teach Laura, learn.

("Oh God, I am so sorry, how often I forget you,
how unappreciative I am.")

Don't teach Laura, learn.

("Please Lord, help me stay open and receptive.")

I prayed for humility, to trust and feel the presence of my Spiritual Master with me. I prayed to learn to do my part to stay in remembrance of God's love and move gratefully and gracefully through my karma. My wish was to be grateful for the painful lessons and not forget God in the happy times.

I learned I was on a floor with other heart patients. Friday morning after another 6 a.m. blood draw, more checks from the nurses and an unhealthy breakfast, I was left to my own devices. I was somewhat mobilized by the rolling IV pull so I decided to explore the territory. Trying to figure out how to modestly clasp the ridiculous rear-end open design of my hospital gown, I strolled with the IV pull around the floor to stretch my legs. I discovered the room where the teletech views the heart telemonitors. I chatted with the reader and watched in fascination at the dozen or so streams of beeps and graphs reading each patient's telemonitor. I watched the graph of my own heartbeat in wonder at the mystery of what was going on inside me.

Later that night my nurse appeared quite suddenly and inquired, "How are you feeling?"

"Fine," I responded. I was brushing my tangled hair.

"You're sure you're feeling okay?" Then I noticed her quizzical expression.

"You just had an episode of ventricular tachycardia. It was detected on your heart monitor."

"Oh. What does that mean?"

"V-Tack is where the heart races very rapidly for several seconds, or longer, in which case you can pass out due to lack of oxygen. If it continues, it can be very serious. The episode was detected on the telemonitor attached to your chest. It was brief, only about nine seconds."

"I did not even notice."

I didn't think much of it. I mean, I didn't feel anything so why should I be alarmed? What I didn't learn until later is that V-Tack can be fatal. I didn't even comprehend that the blood clot could have killed me, nor that the clot and V-Tack might be related to the chf. In my weakened condition, that walk on the beach with Mina had put my heart under tremendous stress.

These incidents prompted the cardiologist on call to seek aggressive measures. That Saturday he came to do his daily rounds, briefly examined me and informed me he was going to schedule surgery the following week to put in a pacemaker. The concept of surgery and a device being implanted just above my chest that would implement an electrical shock should my heart rate drop or drastically change was horrifying to me! I was astounded by the doctor's attitude! He did not ask me, or give me much explanation. He simply informed me of this surgical procedure that he already scheduled for me on Tuesday. When I simply replied "no," it was his turn to be shocked.

"It's your choice, but I have an obligation to inform you that you are endangering yourself by refusal and you'll need to sign a statement saying that you are refusing my recommendation."

"Fine," I said, and he huffed out.

I was furious and upset. How dare he! I didn't even feel that sick. I wanted a second opinion. I was upset that my cardiologist was out of town and I couldn't reach her. I certainly didn't feel sick. Why did I need to have surgery?

The next day the same cardiologist was on call and he stopped in for his daily visit. Having slept on it we both seemed a bit more prepared to attempt to understand one another better. I listened to the reasons why he felt a pacemaker was necessary. So far so good till he compared me to the equivalent of a cigarette smoker who had cancer and decided to continue smoking after being informed of the risks, putting his own life in jeopardy. This was a *very bad analogy* to give to a proud and egotistical holistic health healer!!! I was even more furious and upset than before and demanded a second opinion.

Through the breath, I release my stress.

("I'm so pissed off; what an unfeeling moron.")

Through the breath, I release my stress.

("Okay, I'm not that pissed off. He's just trying to do his job, the best he can. He wasn't trained in people skills; give the guy a break.")

Through the breath, I release my stress.

("I'm going to stay calm; everything is in God's hands. I'm in God's hands; everything is alright.")

The mantra helped me redirect the wave of stress that was pulsing through my body. I drank the air and began to relax. For twenty years I had practiced the belief that I could heal my body with natural non-invasive means. What was happening here? Why wasn't it working? What was I doing wrong?

I didn't see anymore of that on-call cardiologist. I was happy about that. The next day, first thing Monday morning, the director of cardiology came in to see me. Dr. Johnson was direct and looked me in the eyes when he spoke. I liked him right away. He listened. I wondered if he'd been warned I was difficult. He did not convey the opinion about an urgent need for a pacemaker. Good. I was relieved. However after the three episodes of V-Tack, he wanted to up the pills and rattled off that same long list of meds that the gloom and doom doctor had wanted me to start on. This time I acquiesced. It felt like a compromise to saying no to the pacemaker. I was not going to consent to such a drastic measure without consulting with Dr. Guarneri and my friend Steve and not without a lot more research to find out the stuff they didn't tell me about having a foreign device in my body. Why was he so serious? I wasn't going to drop dead tomorrow. Sure, I was a bit weak and tired, but for the most part I felt fine. Why such drama? How was it I could feel fine and have such a serious condition? That was simply incongruous. *They* must be wrong. In the hospital I remained self-protective and hyper-vigilant, but I had to admit the drugs started to make me feel better. Maybe there was something to this pharmaceutical stuff and the western medical process. Most of my doctors were brilliant; that was clear. They were trying their best to help me. After four days, I was more stabilized and was happy to be released and head home.

Dr. Guarneri returned from her speaking engagement and with her input and opinions from two other M.D.s, healers and other friends in the medical profession, I decided not to have the surgery to install the pacemaker. There were many other factors that came into play in making this decision—my petite physical size, my current stamina, my emotional and mental state and my incorporation of alternative healing modalities. Then I had a frightening and freeing epiphany. "Western medicine is as uncertain as everything else in this world. People live when they should die, die when they should live, for no clear reasons. How *dare* the gloom-and-doom doctors predict that I would die without a pacemaker and an extensive list of heart medications!"

My body did not feel like it was dying. Though my stamina was low, I felt much life force and health in my body and believed that a procedure like that would do more harm than good. I couldn't wrap my mind around the idea of a two-and-a-half-inch diameter pacemaker under my skin that could without warning knock me onto the ground with an electric shock. Having chf is like being on a slow boil. The body/mind keeps adapting to its shifting limitations. I had no external objectivity and no partner to daily reflect to me the slow deterioration of my condition. I attributed and reasoned my fatigue due to overwork and stress.

I was now fully steeped into the world of western medicine. I was amazed at the inhuman fast pace of it, the cold insensitivity, the seeming 'automatic pilot' of the doctors and nurses. This was a foreign world of forbidden territory that I had managed to hide away from all my life. Why was there not soft music, quiet and the fragrance of aromatherapy filling the atmosphere? Why did they not understand that it was essential to have windows that could open so you could breathe fresh air to get well? Why did they not have fresh live foods that were nourishing to the body? Why was everyone talking about my symptoms and not questioning how to find a cure? And why was everyone in such a hurry? Where were they going? Was it really that urgent?

When I arrived home there was much to digest. It was as if my brain was on overload. I couldn't make sense of it all. I pulled Shakespeare's "Hamlet" off my shelf of plays. It had oftentimes provided comfort when my emotions made no sense. I knew the passage I was looking for:

> *"Why, looke you now, how unworthy a thing you make of me: you would play upon mee; you would seeme to know my stops: you would pluck out the heart of my Mysterie; you would sound mee from my lowest Note, to the top of my Compasse: And there is much Musicke, excellent Voice, in this little Organ, yet cannot you make it speak. Why do you thinke, that I am easier to bee played on, then a Pipe? Call me*

what instrument you will, though you can fret me, you cannot play upon me."

Hamlet, III:2

I felt played upon. I was just one of 60+ patients on two floors that had to be hurriedly needled for blood twice a day, photocopied, pressurized, pumped, weighed and prodded. How fast could you get it done without making eye contact, or noticing the person might be scared or in pain? There was a human being with feelings in utter amazement at this whirlwind of activity who did not want to be there! I felt manipulated and victimized, alternating with surrender, acceptance and spiritual awe at the magnificence of a perfection being played out far beyond my comprehension. I did not understand this western medical system. The pace was so fast and furious. I learned to respect the tremendous stress and workload these medical professionals were carrying, but it was all so confusing. How was such an environment supposed to help people heal?

My moods vacillated wildly. Often I felt peaceful, but this was interspersed with great episodes of grief, primarily over feeling the increase of physical limitations, which required greater neediness and dependency upon others. I had to ask for more help.

"Please drive me to the store, bring my groceries upstairs, just throw in a load of laundry while you're here." These were such little things that felt huge in the asking whenever a friend might drop by. More often than not, when an offer was made, I responded with, "No, I'm fine," bargaining in my mind that I had to 'save up' the favors for something really big and important if something more serious were to happen. I was fearful that if I couldn't give back people would stop wanting to help me. I'd run out of favors to call in. My outward high self-esteem was a cover up for a deeper level of subtle low self-esteem. I was sure people would really find me just another burden in their already burdened lives. There would be no gain in serving me, and so that old familiar fear of abandonment in my neediest of times would, in fact recur. It was a stark realization and I was too vulnerable to know what to do with it.

The improvement with the new pills gave me hope. It was a surprise, and a relief, but a temporary respite. Several months went by. During this time I increased my sessions for more extensive work with an acupuncturist. It seemed the only accessible alternative that might have enough impact to stimulate my tired heart. I always hated the needles but was willing to endure anything if it could get to the root cause of the problem. The sessions were always potent. At my next echocardiogram my ef had dropped to a mere 16%. How did that happen? I was doing acupuncture twice, sometimes three times a week! It would always give me a temporary lift, but the results were obviously short lived. What if I stepped it up and went every day, or every other day? But I couldn't endure the thought of such frequency with the needles. So far I could find nothing powerful enough to kick my heart into gear.

I was tired all the time, but still seeing clients for counseling and occasionally putting my hands on them. My clients didn't know I had heart failure and I didn't tell them. I knew I had no business running energy into others in my condition but there was now a growing concern about finances. I was scarcely able to work, my practice was dwindling down to a trickle and now there were medical expenses and dealings with the mysterious ways of insurance companies to figure out. Hundreds of bills arrived weekly with incomprehensible strange codes that were impossible to decipher no matter how long I stared at the page. I began to refer out my energy healing clients and kept my practice more limited to spiritual counseling. I began to look ashen and I had no appetite for food, ever. My spirit was strong, my attitude positive and I bore the aura of the spiritual challenges I was enduring. Often others remarked how "good" I looked, which contributed nicely to the distorted perspective of my physical state.

LAURA L. FINE

Helplessly I am swept up into the eye of a hurricane of events beyond my control.
I fight for my life in vehement refusal to surrender to the feelings of powerless helplessness.
My primitive instinct says I will not give in to the feelings of helplessness .
Here is how I resist them ...

_____

_____

_____

_____

_____

_____

_____

_____

_____

_____

_____

_____

_____

_____

_____

The images above are an invitation to self-reflect, explore and discover more of the depths of your soul's mysterious beauty. You may wish to utilize the space above to respond to the image, designed to stimulate your creative subconscious mind. Taking a few minutes to journal your response to the thought, invites an opportunity to deepen your contact with your loving spiritual nature.

LAURA'S NEW HEART — Always Beepng

Weary of battle, I'm ready to experience something different. I agree to open my mind, my body and my breath to the full emotional range of notes that resonate the sensations of helplessness in my being.
As I enter the storm what rises up in me is...

_____

_____

_____

_____

_____

_____

_____

_____

_____

and I discover...

_____

_____

_____

_____

_____

_____

_____

_____

_____

_____

Chapter Three: *Sodi Water*

As time went on, I gained water weight, but lost muscle mass as it was no longer possible to exercise. I didn't have the breath for it. My heart could not pump the fluid out of my lungs, stomach and liver, which made it difficult to breathe and created a constant state of mild nausea. By early afternoon I had to take a breath in the middle of every sentence. Speaking on the phone was especially fatiguing. I forced myself to cook and eat healthy food, but it was increasingly difficult to find the energy to cook and always challenging to eat past the nausea. Mina would come by often, bringing wonderful home-cooked meals and coax me to eat while we watched hour after hour of the "Mahabarat" on videotape. This illness is not linear. Some days would be good and I would think, "Oh, this metabolic typing diet is working, I'm getting better," only to be followed by days where I could hardly breathe or walk upstairs and had a good deal of physical pain and discomfort.

As I continued my research, the number of "alternative" treatments was absolutely overwhelming. Which one should I choose? Which one would work? I had limited time and resources. I would have to choose a path and follow it. I had faith that if I did my part—physically, emotionally and mentally to get better, if it was my destiny to heal, I would be led down a path that would complete the healing. If I were not destined to heal, well, I would be confined to living a very different lifestyle. Perhaps that would not be so bad.

I learned about a famous cardiologist from Mexico City, Dr. Sodi-Pallares. Dr. Guarneri brought him to San Diego as a guest presenter and I listened in wonder to his simple treatment for chf. In case after case, the results had been successful. Dr. Sodi was warm, spiritual and brilliantly creative. He was working at healing the heart with natural methods! I was thrilled. For the first time I was hearing a cardiologist speak about how to actually heal the cause of the problem, not just treat the symptoms. He was talking about how to *reverse congestive heart failure, not just coronary artery disease* which I did not have. Dr. Sodi addressed the biochemistry of how to get the electrical chemical mechanism of the heart to begin pumping without pharmaceuticals. I was excited! Perhaps his method would actually heal my heart! I implemented his diet plan ingesting no more than 1 gram of sodium per day. I looked up the sodium content of every piece of food on the plate before I put it into my mouth. Perhaps this would be the key to my healing; balance the sodium/potassium levels in the body to jumpstart the natural electrical pump that had somehow been damaged. The proper balance would kick it back into gear and the natural healing mechanism of the body could then take it from there. I implemented even more dietary restrictions, but no matter, his theory made sense. His polarizing solution had been around since the 1940s, although used primarily to stabilize heart attack and stroke victims. In emergency rooms around the world, it was nicknamed "Sodi water," after him. I believed this might be the key that would heal me.

Some weeks went by. I was hoping the hospital would approve the implementation of his treatment plan, a simple IV solution of potassium chloride/glucose and insulin. I could purchase the electro-magnetic field mattress to use at home while sleeping, and I could certainly adjust to maintain the 1 gram of sodium per day diet. I waited anxiously for approval from the hospital to begin the IV's of Dr. Sodi's solution, but the weeks of red tape seemed to drag on forever. I tried not to badger Dr. Guarneri but I was impatient. I had no time to waste. My condition was not improving. It was deteriorating. I had to take whatever action I could. This treatment made so much sense to me. I felt that if anything could reverse my heart failure, it would be this. I called clinics all over the U.S. and combed the Internet, trying to find a facility in the U.S. that already worked with Dr. Sodi's treatment. No success. I did not want to go to Tijuana or Mexico City. It was a long trip to a dirty city, and I was extremely feeble and vulnerable. What was I going to do? Were they just going to let me die? Why couldn't they see that my life was ticking by! Maybe I was simply being the over-dramatic theater queen, and I really wasn't that sick. It was all so very confusing.

Around mid-October, after much wrestling in my own mind, I decided to make the trip to Mexico City for his treatment. At least this way I would get the best. Dr. Sodi himself would be treating me. The idea of going to a high-altitude, polluted city where I didn't speak the language was far from appealing. In fact it was frightening in my weakened state, but doing nothing was even scarier. I was impatient.

It is not in my nature to sit, wait and be passive about solving my problems. When I see a problem, I just do what needs to be done to take care of it best I can. If I didn't get well it would not be for lack of trying. I was tired of being sick and tired. I wanted to get better. I *had* to get better. It was getting harder and harder to work. My energy was waning. My emotional moods were extreme. Some days I felt peaceful and accepting. Other days I was despairing and self-pitying.

This trip was another first. I had never been to Mexico City. Who would help care for me, translate for me, make such a commitment of time and money? Both my sister and my sister-in-law offered to accompany me. I did not feel comfortable pulling my sister out of her busy life and my sister-in-law was not someone I was close to, but if I had no other options I would take her up on her offer.

I met Mireya through Dr. Guarneri's conference at Scripps hospital.

LAURA'S NEW HEART — Sodi Water

She had come to the conference to meet Dr. Sodi and learn how he was utilizing electro-magnetism in his therapy. Mireya, Cuban born and fluent in Spanish is a researcher of Electro-magnetic Field Therapy, which is a key part of Dr. Sodi's treatments. Her personality was warm and lighthearted, she was intuitive and bright. We immediately became friends. On a lark I called her to tell her of my plan to go for Dr. Sodi's treatment. I asked her if she was interested in accompanying me. She was thrilled at the idea and said she could use the opportunity to learn about Dr. Sodi's use of electro-magnetic fields in healing for her own research in the same field. Miraculously, her schedule opened. She was happy to assist in my care and to translate and refused to let me pay her airfare. How on earth did that happen? It was as if she had been dropped out of the heavens. What choreography! Mireya stepped into my life at the exact moment of need. It was astounding.

Upon our arrival amidst the crowds and noise of Mexico City, a friend of a friend appeared out of nowhere to meet us at the airport. He had a wheelchair and supplemental oxygen in tow for me. I smiled inwardly at how cared for I felt. Support showed up at every turn to help me through my karma. Feelings of gratitude and humility increased as detail after detail fell seamlessly into place. The man drove Mireya and me to our hotel.

My time in Mexico was a wondrous mixed bag. The city itself was uncomfortable, polluted, crowded, and dirty, and the 7500-foot altitude made it even more difficult to breathe and talk. Yet the people were loving, humanistic, compassionate and generous, making eye contact with kindness and ease. At the clinic, the doctors and staff made me one of the family. The language barrier never stopped them from kissing and hugging me and trying to understand and fulfill my every want and need. Dr. Sodi did a thorough examination and EKG. He immediately started me on his polarizing solution. I sat for six hours on a magnetic mattress, with an IV in a vein, dripping insulin, potassium chloride and glucose. It felt wonderful.

The first day was magnificent. The solution felt like manna from heaven. Perhaps this treatment would work! I could go back to the states and post a message on the chf web site message board. I would tell everyone about this amazing treatment. I would be especially gratified to have that jerk who made fun of me about my alternative choices read about how I got well! Statistically their track record for success with this treatment was extremely good. The doctors here were confident and thorough, the atmosphere absolutely uplifting. I felt hopeful. The second and third days were pure hell. I got horrifically sick, my blood pressure dropped, I was vomiting and white as a sheet. I got scared.

I am safe, it's only change.

("Oh God, I want to go home.")

I am safe, it's only change.

("Okay, God lives here too, in Mexico City, in this little clinic, in the hearts of these people who can barely understand me.")

I am safe, it's only change.

("I don't know anything, I don't understand anything and it's okay.

"There is a Divine plan unfolding here. I don't know what it is, but inwardly I am with my Spiritual Master, I am with God, I am safe, it's only change on the outside. Inside, I am being held by you.")

This was the first time it actually registered that I might die from this illness and even more horrifying to think that I might die in Mexico City. "I am safe. It's only change. Even if I die, if I lose this body, I am safe it's only change." I was so weak, my heart was so weak, how much of this could I take? There was nowhere to go, no one to call. Just go inside, inside to my own heart and lose my mind in the leelas of Radha Krishn.

LAURA'S NEW HEART — Sodi Water

According to the doctors, I probably was suffering from "Montezuma's Revenge." They gave me parasite medicine. The next day I began to feel better. Thank God. Daily Dr. Sodi-Pallares would take time to run an EKG and examine me. His cook would bring me a vegetarian, no-sodium breakfast and lunch. Fresh squeezed juices and fruits and a loving warm environment were healing to my heart and mind. How different, this humble little run down clinic was from the massive technologies of the cold American hospital. My heart began to open. My defenses were so low I could do nothing but trust and feel grateful for the merciful presence of God's love. I felt the warm presence of my Spiritual Master very near me, knowing that he was hearing my prayers to feel his love and was ˜keenly aware of everything that was happening to me. In my mind I kept telling him, "This is so hard, it's so hard, it's so hard." Then I would feel his love fill my heart with peace and strength. I let go and learned to endure and trust the process as it unfolded. By the fourth day I started to improve. Daily I got stronger. "It's working!"

Dr. Sodi and Laura in Mexico City

After seven days, Mireya had to return to the States. I was concerned because Dr. Sodi and Dr. Aguilar, Dr. Sodi's associate, were the only two English speakers at the clinic. Dr. Aguilar generously invited me to move from the hotel to her home after Mireya left. That was another first. My doctor was inviting me to stay with her during the course of my treatment! Her generosity and kindness touched me deeply. It was a gift on so many levels. I felt safe in her care and we had a wonderful time together. The only formidable drawback was the five-flights of stairs up to her apartment. This took about fifteen minutes with many rest stops along the way.

I didn't speak to anyone aside from Dr. Sodi and Dr. Aguilar, and that was okay with me. I enjoyed the solitude. I meditated, prayed, reviewed my life, thought about unfinished business. I felt the consolation of my contact with my spiritual Master and had the great privilege of speaking to him from time to time on the phone at the ashram in Texas.

Keeping my mind positively engaged was a challenge. I had only brought spiritual reading along with me, but at times it was too difficult to focus inward in this manner. I wanted a distraction. Dr Aguilar had an English version of *Shogun* on her shelf. Perfect. When I couldn't focus on anything else I passed the time reading *Shogun*. It kept my mind off my own battle.

After the second week of treatments I was able to slowly climb the five flights of stairs to Dr. Aguilar's apartment without stopping to rest. What a feat! It was evident my life force was increasing, but the constant IV sticks day after day made my veins weary and ragged. The days that Dr. Aguilar had to work out of her own office and did not come to the clinic were most difficult. None of the other doctors or nurses had her loving-touch manner of finding a way into my tiny veins. She would stroke my arm gently and speak to me in such a soothing, reassuring voice that I relaxed and trusted that my body could continue to endure the daily invasion of the treatment.

After the second week with my strength improving I wanted to make an Indian dinner for my doctors and nurses. I cooked and we celebrated. It was fun and distracting, but on the surface a certain part of me was 'performing'. Preparing the meal was exhausting, but I kept it hidden. I tried my best to 'perform' the role of ideal patient to cover up the utter fear, helplessness and exhaustion lurking just below the surface. I began to think daily about dying which I found oddly reassuring, curious and inviting to dwell upon.

I reopened Hamlet, seeking his wisdom:

"... to die, to sleepe
No more; and by a sleepe, to say we end
The Heart-ache, and the thousand Naturall shocks
That Flesh is heir too? 'Tis a consummation
Devoutly to be wish'd.

I too had begun to find myself sometimes entertaining the wish for death to come. It scared me.

To die to sleepe,
To sleepe, perchance to Dream; I, there's the rub,
For in that sleepe of death, what dreams may come,
When we have shuffled'd off this mortal coil,
Must give us pause.

I had full faith that wherever I would be after death would not be terrible, but I wasn't so sure about how bad the dying process could be.

There's the respect
That makes Calamity of so long life:

For who would bear the Whips and Scornes of time,
The Oppressors wrong, the poore mans Contumely,
The pangs of disprz'd Love, the Law's delay,
The insolence of Office, and the Spurnes
That patient merit of the unworthy takes,

How great was this life after all? All these struggles and disappointments, even the successes seemed so meaningless now. Whatever I had achieved would be forgotten, become a slow distant memory like all those I knew who had died before me.

When he himself might his Quietus make
With a bare Bodkin?

I could not conceive of suicide. That was out of the question. And even with all my spiritual awareness, death was still such a vast unknown. What would it really be like to leave all this behind?

Who would these Fardles bear
To grunt and sweat under a weary life,
But that the dread of something after,
The undiscovered Country, from whose Born
No Traveller returns, Puzzels the will,
And makes us rather bear these ills we have,
Then fly to others that we know not of.

Would I really miss this life? How much more suffering would there continue to be in this body? What if I could not endure it?

Thus Conscience does make Cowards of us all,
And thus the Native hew of Resolution
Is sicklied o're, with the pale cast of Thought,

LAURA'S NEW HEART — Sodi Water

And enterprizes of great pith and moment,
With this regard their C urrents turne away,
And loose the name of Action.

Hamlet III.1

Was there an obvious answer I was not seeing, an action I was not taking, something I was avoiding? Was I losing my mind? I felt frozen in time and apathetic. It took great force of will to forge ahead. How would I find that will inside myself?

The plan had been for me to stay and receive treatment for a month. After two and a half weeks my veins were so collapsed, the catheter would not go in. Dr. Aguilar had been away several days. The other doctor stuck me a half dozen times, trying to get a vein, until I finally burst into tears and begged her to stop. I couldn't take any more. My arms were sore and beat up. I decided it was time to come home. I knew my healing was not complete, but I felt stronger, my breathing was easier, and the EKG showed positive results.

I returned home. I was happy to speak English again. I knew my spiritual Master was leaving shortly for India and would not return for many months. I was longing to see him. I felt desperate to see him. I was afraid it might be my last opportunity that I could die before he returned next from India. As I was feeling much improved, the day after my return from Mexico, I got on a plane and went to the ashram in Austin for three days of heaven that lifted my spirits, calmed my mind and eased my fears.

The plane ride back from Austin was tough. I was retaining a great deal of fluid and having difficulty breathing again. Immediately upon my return my condition worsened. The next day I called Dr. Guarneri.

"Come in to the hospital and see me this evening. I want to do an echo on you."

She was as anxious and hopeful as I to see whether Dr. Sodi's treatment showed visible results. The echocardiogram report showed the ejection fraction a disheartening 16%. I knew from how I felt that I was not in good shape but was hoping it was just tiredness from the trip. I'm sure it was apparent in how I looked—pale, weak, and breathless—that I was again in heart failure. I rationalized that the hardships of travel had undone the improvements I'd made from Dr. Sodi's treatment.

"I want to check you back into the hospital." I was not ready to give up. I was adamant about continuing his polarizing solution.

"I improved in Mexico, surely I could improve here in the States if you just give me the same treatment plan. In fact it would be even better because I won't have the hardship of the living conditions, the toll of travel and strange food taxing my system. Can't you please get them to approve this treatment?"

I pleaded with Dr. Guarneri to administer the polarizing solution. I needed her abilities and knowledge. Without her guidance and expertise I would be lost. There was nothing else out there I had found that could heal me. If she took this away, how was I going to get well? She pleaded with me to go through the protocol testing for heart transplantation. I offered her a deal. "Treat me with Dr. Sodi's polarizing solution and I will see the heart transplant doctor for a consultation."

"I'll be right back," Dr. Guarneri said." She left me in the treatment room and dashed out to phone the Director of Cardiology, Dr. Johnson. It seemed like my only trump card. Everyone was so adamant about this stupid heart transplant idea, I would just have to play along till they all got it that I could heal this way. I had to exhaust all alternative options. I had to be absolutely sure I had done everything I could to heal myself safely. Cut my chest open and pluck out my heart! I don't think so, how could they push this on me?! Were they nuts? What were they thinking? Dr. Guarneri recognized this part of me and fought hard to find a way to save my life within the context of this range of my belief system. I felt her frustration. She did not agree with all my choices, but she respected them. I recognized in her a kindred spirit, one who honored the mystery of healing. She held the space for the possibility that perhaps my intuition might be right, that just because she was a doctor, she did not have all the answers. I'm sure I put her through her own angst about my choices, but she supported me without judgment and did her best to keep me alive. I also felt angry. Didn't they realize I was dying and I was trying to get well? Why was there adversity about my trying to save my life through a simple benign polarizing solution? They had nothing to compromise but their own desire to control and judge what they thought was the most medically appropriate protocol, the almighty pharmaceutical. They wanted to keep me in the box of traditional treatment. Dr. Guarneri was my saving grace. She knew that my lessons, whatever they were had to somehow include a way of feeling in control of my own healing process. Perhaps the loss of control was so overwhelming that I had to grasp at straws just to hang on.

She returned with an announcement, "Okay, we can do it, I got the okay, but I want to check you into the hospital right now." I broke down in tears. I felt a mixture of dread at having to endure another hospitalization, gratitude that I could continue Dr. Sodi's treatment, and fear about my deteriorating condition. There was also the enormous sadness that I had put myself through such a wearying physical, emotional and financial expense traveling to Mexico City in order to achieve a simple alternative healing arrangement with a western medical facility in my own backyard. I couldn't help but wonder whether the hardship of travel to Mexico added injury to my heart. I wanted to blame someone at my own hospital for not agreeing to give me the solution sooner. Why did I have to endure all of that just to get someone to listen to me! I didn't understand. I was overwhelmed by Dr. Guarneri's willingness to fight so hard for me. I wondered that she had her own curiosity of what actually brings about healing. I knew she believed strongly in the placebo affect, the power of the mind. Because my desire and belief in this treatment was so strong, perhaps she kept a place open in her own mind for the possibility that it could work. I didn't know for sure and she never said. Dr. Guareneri was humble enough to respect my inner voice and open to the mysterious and unexplainable ways of healing. She got it that the only way for me to consider a heart transplant was to let me exhaust every other possible alternative. She risked her reputation by prescribing a treatment everyone else in the medical department felt was useless. She did it for me. I had no words to articulate my silent gratitude. I barely had breath or energy to convey my emotions anyway. I only hoped she understood. I felt I had won a battle, I had won my life. Now I could really focus on healing, resting, eating properly and growing stronger.

In my weakened condition, my heart was not pumping well and needed another IV of diuretics to drain my lungs and visceral organs of excess fluids. When I became somewhat stabilized, they released me from the hospital. Dr. Guarneri ordered an oxygen machine for me to use at home. Good, oxygenating the body would help ease the work of my tired heart and be good for my entire system. I named the machine R2-D2 for its resemblance and spoke to it with fond appreciation as I hooked up morning and night to soak in its life force.

I started receiving my IV transfusions of Dr. Sodi's solution at the transfusion clinic. This was a first for the hospital cardiology clinic, offering an alternative healing polarizing solution! I was happy. I would receive treatment as an outpatient twice a week, for six hours a day. This would be more tolerable for my tired veins, and more conducive to adapting my body to homeostasis. I was convinced that in three to four months time, my heart would have all the juice it needed to respond to the chemistry of the solution, gain strength and heal itself.

I had been instructed to weigh myself daily to watch for sudden fluid weight gain. My normal weight most of my adult life hovered around 108-110 pounds. Now it seemed to fluctuate between 99 and 101. One morning when mounting the scale I noticed an increase of a few pounds. It brought me to recall my experience in San Antonio, when I stepped on the scale and it said 118, instructing the nurse that her scale was ten pounds off. I laughed hysterically all day at the reflective realization that their scale was absolutely correct. I was completely unaware that I had gained ten pounds of water weight. Ten pounds and not notice?! Me? That was astounding, and I found it hysterically funny. All that pride and ego around being so in touch with my body was completely flattened again. Any and everything I thought I had control over or pride in was being stripped away. What an awesome teacher this heart failure is. All that will be left of me can only be my eternal soul. Anything and everything temporary and transitory—all my beliefs and concepts about how things work—were destroyed, one piece at a time. It was relieving actually, hysterically funny and relieving. I didn't have to try to make sense out of anything anymore, because nothing ever would make sense!!! I knew there was a perfection playing out, but it was far beyond me to think I could ever grasp even the smallest corner of God's wisdom and choreography. I was simply grateful to feel His love and amusement as He continually enticed me to come closer to Him, think of Him, trust Him, love Him.

Those twice-weekly six-hour stints lying still on a hospital bed provided time for observation, reflection and surrender. The pace of my life slowed down considerably. I saw the meaninglessness of conflict all around me. I recognized how many precious moments I'd wasted in selfishness, moments that could have been used to think of God, to love God, and other people.

Sir, in my heart there was a kind of fighting,
That would not let me sleepe;

...let us know,
Our indiscretion sometimes serves us well,
When our dear plots do pale, and that should teach us,
There's a Divinity that shapes our ends,
Rough-hew them how we will."

Hamlet, V.2

I wanted to see the perfection of this dance that I could neither control nor comprehend. I started looking at people, really deeply looking. I saw myself in everyone around me. I felt as though their fears, burdens and stresses far outweighed my own. I felt so aware of God's presence that I did not feel the loneliness I observed in so many others around me.

After a few weeks of the polarizing transfusions, I felt some improvement again, but it was a roller coaster effect that went up and down. This was followed by another few weeks in and out of the hospital in varying degrees of heart failure.

My sister called daily to check on me. My friend Beth came down on weekends from L.A. to make me laugh and lecture me about listening to my doctors. She and many others tried time and again to discuss heart transplant with me. What was their problem? Why couldn't they see and support the choices I was making? I couldn't understand it and I was furious at all of them. I wouldn't listen. I was tired of everyone pushing "transplant" at me. I wanted to stay focused on getting well and believed that, over time, Dr. Sodi's treatment in conjunction with a strict diet and biweekly acupuncture could reverse this illness. It was hard enough doing all this on my own. I wanted their support and belief in what I was doing, but it wasn't forthcoming from any direction. I had to give this treatment everything I could until my heart pump would "kick in" and I would heal. If this didn't work…well, I would cross that bridge when and if I came to it.

I purchased one of Dr. Sodi's magnetic mattresses. They shipped it from Mexico. I continued the six-hour IV drip treatments twice a week for the next two months, and at night I slept four to six hours on the mattress. The magnetism felt deeply consoling and womb-like. I'd fall asleep to the soothing chanting of God's name.

A prophet has come. He tells you, "Stop what you are doing right now! Stop reading, note the time, write it down, right this minute, write this minute, the exact hour, the exact minute of this moment.

Noted _____...

Now he tells you, "In twenty-four hours, you will die."

I take his words deeply in. I reflect. In twenty-four hours I will die.

What I will do with this time is...

_____

_____

_____

_____

_____

_____

_____

_____

_____

_____

The images above are an invitation to self-reflect, explore and discover more of the depths of your soul's mysterious beauty. You may wish to utilize the space above to respond to the image, designed to stimulate your creative subconscious mind. Taking a few minutes to journal your response to the thought, invites an opportunity to deepen your contact with your loving spiritual nature.

LAURA'S NEW HEART — Sodi Water

LAURA L. FINE

Laura in San Diego at 92 pounds

Chapter Four: *Denial*

Don't   *D*

   Even   *E*

    kNow   *N*

     I   *I*

      Am   *A*

       Lying   *L*

I was released from the hospital just in time for Thanksgiving. My brother checked in regularly from Cincinnati by phone. My sister came in from New York to spend the holiday with me. Though we had spoken almost daily by phone, she now saw close up how sick I really was. Nonetheless we had a wonderful time together, sitting on the beach, reading books. She taught me how to increase my protein intake on a vegetarian diet. She spent the week cooking sumptuous meals, trying to fatten me up, but I had no appetite. I had become so used to the nausea I scarcely noticed it. I just knew I didn't want to eat.

It had been several weeks since I had begun to receive Dr. Sodi's intravenous polarizing solution treatments. Now my sister took the opportunity of her visit to push me to see the transplant doctor for an evaluation. Since that was my end of the bargain, I finally agreed to go. Though inwardly the heels of my mind were resolutely dug into the ground, I forced myself to keep this agreement.

Mentally I had the whole thing pre-planned, what I would say to these torturers who wanted to cut my chest open just to make money. I simply decided what I would refuse to hear. I was trying to protect my mind from those who doubted my ability to heal myself naturally. I believed their doubts would harm my own faith. I felt their negative thoughts would destroy my focus and belief in the healing protocol that I had chosen for myself. I was Joan of Arc on a solo mission, a martyr, superior to their level of understanding. Even if no one else believed in me or thought I was crazy, I would do everything I could to fight for my life in the way I thought I could heal. I felt vulnerable and defensive. I convinced myself I was going to this appointment out of obligation. However, a tiny corner of my mind wanted to go, the part that could not ignore the opinions of my sister and Dr. Guarneri, both whom I respected. Then of course there was the factor of my own deteriorating condition. I prepped Melanie in the car on the way to the doctor's office. "If you want to know more details about heart transplant you can ask all the questions you want after I leave the room."

I went on the attack the moment the door shut in the private treatment room. I said to Joan, the nurse and transplant co-coordinator, "*I don't want to know anything about the procedure of a heart transplant!* I am only here because I am keeping my end of the bargain with Dr. Guarneri. You can ask me any questions you need to ask about my health and I will answer you. I don't want any images or thoughts about heart surgery or transplant in my mind or consciousness. I am doing another treatment right now and I want to keep all my focus and positive thoughts on that treatment."

She was taken aback. I did not learn till much later that most people pray day and night, wait months sometimes years for the chance to get a heart transplant. I was there kicking and screaming that I didn't want one, but I was white as a sheet and obviously (to them) in the throws of heart failure. I was scared, defensive and resistant. I repeated the same story to the transplant doctor when he came into the examining room.

His loud and booming voice extolled facts and statistics that in my opinion had nothing to do with *me*. His impersonal tone affirmed my belief that I was 'unseen' by yet another traditional western medical doctor. He did a brief examination, listened to my heart and asked if I had any questions. I retorted with a flat, "No."

The doctor and nurse tried their best to be calm and understanding. I instantly decided I didn't like the doctor. My sister had a different reaction. She was impressed with both of them. I just wanted out of the room as quickly as possible. Joan the transplant coordinator was kind and gracious, but I decided right away that I did not like the doctor.

It took every ounce of my control to even pretend to be somewhat polite. I asked if he was done then quickly excused myself from the room. Melanie stayed to further question the doctor. Inwardly I was glad, though I could scarcely find space in my mind to admit it to myself. She would think of questions to ask that I was no where near ready to entertain. Then, perhaps on the off chance I ever did need to know anything more, I could ask her.

Why was it no one seemed to understand, support or empathize as to why it was impossible for me to discuss heart transplant? How on earth could I listen to the description of a heart transplant and *heal* at the same time? Cutting my chest open, taking out my heart??? Putting in another one and pumping me full of immune suppressant drugs for the rest of my life? Not being able to go out in public for fear of getting sick all the time? What a way to live. They wanted me to *choose* to live like that?! Were they crazy?! They call that healing?

"*I want not buzzers to infect my ear with pestilent speeches…*" I agreed with Hamlet. Hearing the details would be far too horrifying and vivid in my mind—filling it with images that would be antithetical to my healing. How could they expect me to listen?! Why was it so difficult for anyone to understand this from my perspective?

On the drive home my sister didn't let me off the hook. She confronted me about my defensive rationalization and my close-minded attitude. She was frustrated with my stubbornness. I was not ready to give up on the polarizing solution treatment. No one understood what it was to be in my shoes, in this body except for me. I longed to feel some kind of mysterious emotional support that no human being could have ever provided. I felt very alone, but one thing was certain. Transplant would be the absolute last resort, yet I hadn't given up trying to heal myself.

Each morning I awoke feeling hopeful, as there would be some surge of energy in my body. I would watch, self-observe in my meditations in an effort to notice if the solution was having an effect. My spirits were lighthearted most of the time and I would go about my life with a new thoughtfulness and wonder at the adjustment to my new life style. This slower pace allowed time for self-reflection, introspection and meditation. It was as though I were looking at my body and the world through a window rather than participating in my life. I did not mind. I learned to do chores and errands in the morning during the four hours I had energy. By midday I was spent and by late afternoon, moving my now ninety-eight pound body around the house felt like pulling a fully loaded moving van with a Volkswagen. To get from the couch to the closet, change my clothes and climb into bed took a sheer act of will. Sometimes I would sit on the couch for ten minutes affirming, "You can do it Laura, you can do it, you can make it. You'll feel better in the morning; you always do." Then I would lift myself to standing, take the long twenty-foot hike from living room to bedroom in slow motion, and climb into bed. Amazingly I still did not grasp how sick my body was, how close I was to death.

It was around this time I took a nose-dive. One evening I

hesitatingly paged Dr. Guarneri. Nothing felt that different or unusual. There were no urgent symptoms but something did not feel right. I was surprised with her immediate response. She wanted me to check into the hospital right away. I agreed. I did not feel good, but I didn't understand why. When the cardiologist on call stopped by to check me out he asked if I really thought I needed to be there. I was amazed and befuddled by his question.

"I don't know, you tell me! I don't feel good." Did he think I was faking it, that I was there because I just wanted attention? His attitude was annoying and patronizing. In hindsight I realize that chf is really a deceptive illness. It creeps up on you slowly and subtly and you don't realize its seriousness. Outwardly you appear quite normal to most people, and because my demeanor was so frequently lighthearted, I was often told I looked "good" rather than sick. My spirit did not feel "sick." In fact, most of the time my spirit felt great. It was only my body that didn't seem to match what I was feeling inside. This didn't agree with the New Age concept that body reflects mind and mind reflects body. These two puzzle pieces did not fit together. I remembered my Spiritual Master's words, "You are not the body, you live *in* the body but *you* are not the body." This understanding gave me consolation as I lay in yet another hospital bed with catheters in my arm, IV drips of diuretics and during endless blood draws.

*I am not this body, I live **in** the body,*
but I am not this body.

("I'm scared mom, I'm scared, but I'm glad you're not alive to see me like this. I wouldn't want you to see me like this, but I'm scared mommy."

*I am not this body, I live **in** the body,*
but I am not this body.

("This is so hard, it's so hard, it's so hard.")

*I am not this body, I live **in** this body,*
*but **I** am not this body.*

("It's okay, I'm okay, I can do this. Everything is alright, I can do this.")

Emotionally, how I wanted my mother. The little kid hurting part wanted protective warm and loving motherly arms around me. The grown-up part knew that it was Divine Mother I really wanted.

I was in continual confusion about how physically ill I actually was. My energy would go through erratic spurts. From time to time when I had a really good day or two—when I could be active, even take walks or go out to dinner—I thought I was getting better! Then there would be a subtle shift and I would feel tired. These days I convinced myself I was just being lazy. "If I did my yoga and breathing exercises more diligently I wouldn't have these problems." That was partly denial, but it also reflected my ignorance about the disease of heart failure. I had still not met anyone with heart failure. What did it look like? I surfed the net and read message boards with notes from people who had it, but never spoke with any of them or met them. There was still so much mystery. Who were these people? Why hadn't I ever met them? What did they look like? I started watching people in the grocery stores. That man who was thin and pale, did he have heart failure? Were they all elderly? How could you tell if you passed someone on the street that secretly had heart failure? Were there support groups somewhere? Certainly no one knew that I had anything wrong from looking at me.

Spiritually, I daily contemplated death. No one thought to explain to me what physical dying would or could look or feel like. Perhaps my doctors were afraid to discuss that topic directly. I suppose everyone is different, but I wanted to know. My curiosity about death grew daily, and daily I felt my body moving toward it. Paradoxically I could not sense how intimately closely we were dancing.

Each time my lungs filled up with fluid and breathing became too difficult, I'd go back into the hospital. This time Dr. Guarneri was away on another speaking engagement. Dr. Johnson, the head honcho, came to see me. I was glad to see him again and appreciated his logic and compassion. He ordered a chest x-ray and diagnosed pneumonia. He could not, however, explain the increasingly excruciating pain I was experiencing in one specific spot just below the ribs on the left side of my back. Many tests and several days went by. Trapped in my sickroom, I was starved for fresh air and real food. My long tangled hair felt uncomfortably dirty. I had no strength to wash it and fantasized about chopping it all off. It was challenging enough to be confined in the hospital. Add to that being a vegetarian, and it's like you're from another planet. They would send me a dry baked potato with a plate of canned baked beans. I was nauseous all the time anyway, but trying to get this food down was impossible.

I was pushing to get out of there; I longed to go home, eat healthy food, breathe fresh air, get some sleep and get well! Dr. Johnson finally acquiesced and dismissed me, a bit prematurely in his opinion, as my sodium levels were still low. I left the hospital hoping that the change of environment, fresh air and healthy food would help me heal. The only problem was the pain in my back was increasing. The doctors had no explanation for this. I made up a new affirmation...

Pain is the yellow brick road to my spiritual destination.

("I hate this, I hate this, I hate this...")

Pain is the yellow brick road to my spiritual destination.

("I'm so tired of being in pain, so tired, I just want to die...")

*Pain is the yellow brick road to
my spiritual destination.*

> ("It's all perfect, it's all perfect, everything is okay…this is taking me
> to my spiritual destination, everything is okay.")

Enduring pain sapped the small amount of energy reserve I had left. I felt so weak that washing my hair became a daunting and monumental task. As the days in the hospital trickled by my greasy long hair became an object of fantasy and excitement. I couldn't wait to get free of it. It had been long almost all my life. How short would I cut it? To my shoulders? To my ears? Buzz it all off? The day I got home from the hospital I called the hair salon down the block for an appointment. I had visualized the entire thing. I plodded down the street to the salon. "Cut it all off" was all I said to the hairdresser, and watched with great relief as my years of long locks hit the floor. Somehow it was a symbol of letting go of many things—my vanity and attachment to images of youth and success. I looked in the mirror. I looked different. I wasn't pretty anymore and I didn't care.

Two days later, I did something unimaginable. I turned around and took myself to the hospital to be readmitted. After two days and two nights of no sleep from unbearable pain, I couldn't take it anymore. I felt exhausted and defeated. I just wanted out of pain. I wanted morphine, and they gave me morphine. THAT was a first! I was sitting up in bed and the morphine was administered intravenously. For the first time in my life I felt truly grateful for drugs. Five minutes later I was asleep with my eyes open, still sitting up. I don't know how long I sat like that. I lost all sense of time. When I came to and noticed myself still sitting upright, I laid down, slept through the night and half the next day. The pain continued throughout the duration of my hospital stay. They said it was because of the pneumonia but that didn't make sense to me. How could pneumonia cause such pain in a specific localized spot? No one seemed to know what was causing it. Their only solution was, of course, more painkillers.

After some sleep, I was able to endure a little better. I took another dose of the morphine but didn't like the drowsiness—the way it muddled my mind. Not having a significant other to act as an advocate, I was afraid about what might happen if I couldn't think straight to make crucial decisions. I tried Darvacet and other painkillers. They too made me foggy, so I refused the pills and used breathing techniques and meditation to give me occasional respite. It was more important to me to be alert and aware. I did not trust the impersonal, ever-fluctuating staff of doctors and nurses to recognize, respect, and incorporate my healing systems into my health care.

I walked to the hospital bathroom and looked in the mirror. For forty-five years it had shown me an agile, athletic body crowned by long black hair. Now my muscle tissue was atrophied, my hair was short and grayed, my eyes gaunt, face ashen, back hunched and rounded. I could barely recognize this strange ninety-year old figure looking back at me.

"*To what base uses we may return, Horatio!*" I couldn't seem to get *Hamlet* off my mind.

I observed the progressive decay of my physical body in the mirror, how base this body. I didn't hate myself, but who was myself? This body? Who was she? Who did this belong to? I stared in detached fascination. Inside this shell, I was very alive and conscious.

From time to time I kept up with Dr. Aguilar in Mexico through emails. When she told Dr. Sodi of my pain symptoms, he said I might have had a blood clot in my lung. Because the level of pain in my back was comparable to the pain from the clot I'd had in my leg, I wondered whether this might have been the case. It was another month before the excruciating back pain began to subside.

During those days as I was in such physical agony, I often wanted to be out of my body. I thought frequently about dying. I thought about how my sister and brother would deal with my death, what they might think of my journals and a loving entry I'd written to my brother that I had never shared with him. However, most of me didn't care much about any of that. I focused primarily on my relationship with my spiritual Beloved. Meditating brought reassurance and comfort. The pain was teaching me to focus very deeply, intensely inward. I would visualize Divine leelas of God in loving playfulness. When I was able to mentally accomplish this, the pain would decrease dramatically. I experienced a feeling of *knowing* where I would go after death. Whether true or not, it gave me a tolerance for pain. It was as though my mind was woven into a cycle of *pain, resistance, awareness, surrender, acceptance, focus, comfort,* and *peace.*

Pain, resistance, awareness, surrender.

("There's nothing to hang on to...")

Surrender, surrender, surrender, surrender

("This life does not belong to me...")

Surrender, surrender, surrender, surrender.

("Aaaaahhhh, there's that feeling again, the Grace, thank you, thank you, thank you, thank you.")

Even after the treasure of this understanding, I could not claim to *not* fear death. However, I did find that fear was only present when I gave into the "what ifs"—when wondering how much worse the physical pain might become before death would overtake me. At these times I learned to use my will to force my mind to focus on the joy of being alive in this precious moment. I was growing in my ability to visually focus my mind. What a great opportunity this turned out to be! I began to value the opportunity to love God with each moment, with each breath—clearly aware now that there might not be many of these moments left for me to enjoy His love with awareness and appreciation. I imagined no longer having the burden of a body, and dwelling in the garden of Vrindaban with my Divine Beloved. Sweetness would wash over me. I would feel myself there in that garden in the present moment. Faith grew—faith that this eternal abode of God would one day be my dwelling place, "*if it not be now, yet it will come.*" Somehow God's loving presence would be with me in the transition of death. I trusted that it would be in some manner familiar, not frighteningly foreign. I looked forward to that feeling, to that time.

When I was released from the hospital I went to my chiropractor. An adjustment helped break the pattern of pain and sporadically it began to gradually decrease. My attention turned to daily maintenance. Shopping, cooking and cleaning all had to be done in the morning when I had enough energy to function. It was embarrassing to ask the grocery bagger to carry out my three small plastic food bags to the car, but I had no choice. It was challenging enough to carry my own body. Arriving home, there was the daily deliberation: "What would be easier, one trip up the stairs carrying all three small plastic grocery bags? Or, do I leave the heaviest one at the bottom and muster the strength to tackle the staircase a second time?" After achieving the feat of lifting the groceries onto the counter, I would switch on the oxygen machine, rest a few minutes and catch my breath before putting the groceries away. I padded around the house, dragging forty feet of oxygen tubing behind me, slowly making my way from kitchen to office, bedroom to bathroom, and attending to basic survival housekeeping tasks. Three or four consecutive "bad" days would be followed by two or three "good" days, again providing the disorienting illusion of improvement. Though this cycle repeated itself numerous times I could not identify any consistency, pattern or logic. I continued to assume that I still just hadn't found the right formula/combination of diet/supplements/polarizing solution to establish steady improvement.

I remember a trip to the gas station where I needed to check my oil. When I tried to open the hood of my car, I was so weak I could scarcely raise it. This was frightening. I looked around to be sure no one noticed. It dawned on me that I was vulnerable and could be easy prey. I barely had strength to scream, let alone defend myself should someone approach me with malevolent intentions.

After simple morning errands I was spent. I screened my phone calls because I didn't have the energy or breath to talk on the phone. I listened inwardly, waiting to feel my body's physiological response to the polarizing solution. I could not grasp that I might die soon. I figured I would just have to live a more compromised, rather inactive life. I tried to scan ahead. What would life be like in the long-term, functioning at such a reduced capacity? Would I move in with my sister, move to the ashram? Where would I go? Who would take on the burden of taking care of me?

I kept juggling finances to find a way to survive without bringing in income. Dr. Guarneri suggested I apply for disability. Disability!!? What was she thinking? I wasn't in a wheelchair. I had both my arms and legs. My mind was clear. After a few weeks the idea slowly penetrated. It was true. My practice had dwindled to a trickle. I no longer possessed the stamina to see clients. My savings were flooding through my fingers like water through a sieve. I wondered whether I would be dead before it mattered, or if I lived, *how* I would live with nothing left. I kept busy with paperwork trying to figure out an easier way to build an income. I couldn't figure it out. I had always been great at creative income, but this time I was stumped. Another surrender. I applied for disability. I felt humiliated. I never imagined myself as one of "those" on disability. Here was another recognition of my prejudice and arrogance. I was now one of 'those' as well.

Every Tuesday and Thursday I religiously went to the hospital for my six-hour IV drip treatments. Fortunately Sherri was great with the needles and always managed to get into my tiny and increasingly frazzled veins. On good days, I would feel a bit of a boost from the polarizing solution and think, "hey, it's working, I'm getting better!" These were typically followed by a few bad days. I managed to eke out a few days during Christmas without being in the hospital, and had a joyful time with my spiritual family and loving friends.

There is a cry for help locked inside my throat, buried deep in my chest and belly, held down by my pride. Today I am going to let it speak and it cries out loud saying...

_____

_____

_____

_____

_____

_____

_____

_____

_____

_____

_____

_____

_____

_____

The images above are an invitation to self-reflect, explore and discover more of the depths of your soul's mysterious beauty. You may wish to utilize the space above to respond to the image, designed to stimulate your creative subconscious mind. Taking a few minutes to journal your response to the thought, invites an opportunity to deepen your contact with your loving spiritual nature.

Chapter Five: *I'm Alive, It's a Good Day*

On December 28th, Mary, Alex, Mina and one of my spiritual teachers came to visit. My spiritual teacher took one look at me and said, "Laura, I think you should call your doctor." I knew in my heart that she was right. I didn't look good. I didn't feel good. I picked up the phone with dread, knowing it probably meant another return to the hospital. I was becoming a regular—like one of the locals at the corner coffee shop—but certainly the hospital was not so charming an environment. How many times could I keep this up, these constant forays in and out of the hospital? I was sure my insurance company had me on their secret "I hope she'll hurry up and die list." I called Dr. Guarneri.

Dr. Guarneri didn't hesitate for one moment, "Come to the hospital right away." How did she know? She hadn't even seen me yet. I just figured she had some mysterious 'doctor instinct' and followed her advice. Back I went. The next morning when she came to my bedside on her rounds, she took one look at me and sent me to ICU. Why was she putting me in ICU? ICU only happened in the movies, on television shows when you arrived in an ambulance after being hit by a car. It didn't happen to *me!* That was a first. I had never been in ICU before. I didn't get it. Why? Last night I slept in my own bed—actually on the couch—so I wouldn't have to get up and walk to the bed. But feeling like that wasn't so unusual. I was used to it. That was just how my way of life was now, so why ICU? What had changed from last night to now? I didn't feel any worse than "normal". What was different?

ICU meant more beeps, more tubes hanging out of my arms and every other body part. I grilled every doctor and nurse. What does that machine do? That drug? What are the side-affects? How long will I need to take this? Why? Sometimes I said "no". In ICU I remember feeling absolutely exhausted. I often found myself reporting, "I feel so tired, so tired." I could scarcely keep my eyes open and spent much time in a fluctuating sleep/semiconscious state. I had almost no breath to talk.

The respiratory therapist came by every hour and gave me hits on a special respirator to help me breathe. The oxygen felt delicious. I recall hearing someone say that the lack of oxygen was affecting my mind. What did that mean? I didn't have the strength to inquire, or capacity to figure it out. I remember at one point looking up and seeing my friend Beth sitting in the corner reading a magazine. Why did she drive all the way down from LA again to visit me in the hospital, just to read a magazine? As I looked at her sitting quietly flipping the pages, I had so many mixed feelings. How would I entertain her? I wanted her to talk to me but I could scarcely talk. Why wasn't she doting over me? Yet, even in this state, the idea of someone being there to assist me was foreign and difficult to accept. Perhaps she would distract me from the stress of my surroundings. Was my pride *still* so enormous and my self-esteem still so low that I could not ask for this additional attention? I had to figure she had nothing else to do, so she came to see me. Later she told me that ignoring me was the only way that I would just rest.

It seemed impossible to keep my eyes open. I may have actually been approaching a coma. In a muddled state of consciousness I came to this startling realization, "I think my body is dying and I am still trying to take care of everyone else." The caretaker so deeply ingrained in me just could not let go. Not only that, I was trying to hide my caretaking tendencies from others, but they already knew this about me anyway! Was nothing sacred?

My body had been utterly naked, invaded and exposed. Tubes were inserted, extending in and out of every hole. Where there wasn't a hole, they made one. My emotions were beyond my control. Now even my personality was transparent. There was no private corner left anywhere. With this insight, I didn't even have the energy to cry. I recognized what seemed like an endless depth of increasingly subtle layers of patterned co-dependency at work within me. Something had to shift. I was forced to shift and so I did.

Whoever was on "watch" detail took phone calls and kept visitors away as much as possible. Yet friends continued to bring me food, flowers and love. Healers and body workers showed up in my hospital room to work on me. People I didn't know appeared at my bedside to give me healing touch. Who were they, how did they know? I opened up and let myself receive and receive and receive. It was astounding— more miracles. I laughed and cried and gave thanks. I did not understand why and where they all came from. Yet, their loving touch helped my body release the trauma of continuous invasion that was necessary to keep me alive. There were Pic lines (IV tubes that enter through the arm into the heart), a Swann-Ganz catheter in the neck to test pressures in the heart, blood draws and shots of anticoagulant in the belly, morning and night. I was learning to make my body and mind receptive and accepting. I was helpless, dependent, extremely physically weak and vulnerable. My mind stayed hyper-vigilant, watching every move of the nurses and questioning every doctor.

Laying here in ICU it finally dawned on me. Dr. Sodi's polarizing solution was just not going to work for me. Perhaps it wasn't strong enough. I am sure I was the last one to realize. Everyone else understood the gravity of my condition more than I. This was due to my denial, ignorance of the nature of heart disease, and also fear of the words *"heart transplant"—heart transplant, where they saw your sternum in half, spread your rib cage apart, pluck out your heart and insert another one! I don't think so! How could I possibly let them do that???*

I had lots of preconceptions. I anticipated transplant as a lifelong disability accompanied by negative judgments and pity from others. I feared my immune system being forever compromised, taking hundreds of pills a day, suffering many complications and getting sick all the time. I believed that my life with chf would not necessarily be any better after a heart transplant and could possibly be worse. No doctor was willing to provide a guarantee. I couldn't understand why so many people were adamant that I should put myself through such a horrific procedure when I was sure my life would be so exceedingly compromised. Why not just live with my current limitations without going through all the horror of having my chest cut in half? How would I survive *that?*

My sister flew in from New York. Laying there in ICU, I would occasionally glance through the glass doors of my room into the hallway and see other patients. One young boy about sixteen was wheeled in. He had more tubes going in and out of him than I. I said to my sister, "Just when I start feeling sorry for myself, I see someone who has it much worse than I do."

"Yeah," she said, "But you can do something about it. You can *get a heart transplant!* He has cancer, he can't do that!" Her anger and frustration with me was apparent. I looked over at him. He had to be one of the only ones here who could have an idea about what it was that I was going through. He was going through it too! And it was true, he was dying. In that moment I recognized my deep prejudice toward all those "other people" in hospitals who were diseased, disabled, crippled and critically ill. I never wanted to be like them, I never was one of them; *they* must have done something wrong or bad to get like that. Now my attitude was changing. I wanted to know these people. Who were they? What were their lives before their illness? They were facing death. How did they handle facing death? How did their illness come upon them? Moreover, how was *"I"* like *them?* I looked at the boy with cancer. I had become like him. I was intrigued by the mystery of it all. I saw him with kind eyes.

My spiritual community, teachers and friends helped me hang on through their faith, love and inspiration. I began to understand the words of my Spiritual Master that I had been reading over and over.

"Our Divine Mother knows what is good for every soul and She is caring for you."

("This wheel of life, it is so amazingly beautiful.")

"Our Divine Mother knows what is good for every soul and She is caring for you."

("Every word my Spiritual Master has ever spoken is the truth, it's all so true, it's really true.")

"Our Divine Mother knows what is good for every soul and She is caring for you."

("I am so lucky to know that this is true, so very lucky. This is good for my soul. Everything that has happened, everything that is happening is somehow good for my soul.")

I began to accept and surrender to the process at hand. My greatest defense and ally, my mind, no longer functioned clearly. I let go completely to the doctors and nurses and trusted others to care for me. I was dying. My body was dying. I finally got it. My body was dying. How much time did I have left? How close was my time of death? A few months, a few weeks, a few days?

Dr. Guarneri asked me again, "Would you please just get evaluated for a heart transplant?"

LAURA'S NEW HEART — I'm Alive, It's a Good Day

I surrendered. There was no other recourse. I had tried everything, nothing worked. "Yes."

Dr. Guarneri paused for a moment and held her breath with a stunned expression. Then with an exhale she jumped into action. Perhaps she was afraid I'd change my mind if she took a second breath. Instantly a flurry of activity began all around me. Dr. Guarneri made a dash for the phone and put in the call to Sharp Hospital. My sister started packing my personal belongings and the nursing staff began fussing with tubing. There was a swirl of activity from every direction.

What I didn't realize was that the evaluation for heart transplant would have to be done at Sharp Hospital, not Scripps. This was disconcerting. It meant leaving the familiarity of Scripps and Dr. Guarneri's care. It was 10 p.m. in the evening. Now I was alert, a bit revived from the respiratory therapy and slightly argumentative about having to ride in an ambulance.

"An ambulance? Why? Isn't that a bit dramatic?" I felt okay, my body wasn't in pain. In fact, I was greatly relieved just to have that Swann-Ganz catheter out of my neck. Why couldn't I just ride in the car with my sister to the hospital? Why all this fuss?

"I'm not going to die in the car on the way over, it's only a half hour drive from here," I pleaded.

The doctors refused. It wasn't clear to me whether they were just afraid of the liability or if I was far worse then I knew. Melanie followed, driving my car behind the ambulance, on the way to Sharp Hospital. That was a thirty-minute, one-thousand-dollar limousine ride.

The next morning I woke up in a whole new territory to begin an evaluation for transplant receptivity. Another ICU, a different staff, more machines, lots more tests—even more invasive this time—and another Swann catheter sticking out of my neck. They did an angiogram, which requires a tube to be inserted up through the femoral artery in the groin and into the heart to measure pressure and other information.

In ICU the room was crowded with the latest technology and lots of noise and bustling activity. A portable potty was placed next to my bedside as the extensive hookups limited my range of movement to about two feet. Twice daily I would stand and march in place for ten minutes to slow the atrophy of the muscle mass in my legs.

The nurses amazed me. Their attentiveness to the intricacy of beeps and buttons was unflagging. They gave me more intense doses of diuretics to drain the fluid from my visceral organs, as the heart was too weak to pump it out. Nurse Bridget wanted to insert a catheter so I wouldn't have the extra labor of continually getting up to use the port o'potty next to my bed—to urinate out the fluids draining from my sluggish body as it began to respond to the diuretics.

"No. Don't I have enough tubes in me as it is? I am capable of getting up to sit on the port o' potty. It's right here!"

"Suit yourself. If you change your mind, just let me know. Oh, and by the way, one of these IVs is a diuretic. You're going to have to get up an awful lot to pee if you don't have a catheter in."

Bridget was stubborn and direct. I liked her right away. She explained things to me and gave me the space to decide. After the third time in ten minutes—climbing out of bed, untangling myself from the maze of tubing to make my way to the potty—I inquired, "Does it hurt?"

"No," she said amused, "You're hardly going to feel it go in."

"Have you put these in many people before?"

She gave me a sardonic smile. "Thousands of times Laura. I've been an ICU nurse for 16 years." Before she finished her sentence the catheter was in and I had hardly noticed. We chuckled together. Not only was she angelically compassionate, she and the other ICU nurses were amazing technicians, contending with massive amounts of machinery, computer systems and sterilization with deft expertise. They checked pressures in my heart at least six times daily and changed dozens of feet of tubing attached to the six different IV solutions now circulating throughout my system. I remembered my bullheaded refusal to be zapped by one x-ray, lest it distort the *purity* of my system. How arrogant. How stupid! How humbled I now felt. It was good to feel humble; it took less effort. I observed these merciful masters, on their feet for twelve hours straight, attempting to be cheerful while working to keep me alive, always aware that one error could jeopardize my life. How on earth did they do it? And on top of all that, how did they cope with the heightened fears and personality quirks of each individual patient? How did they hold that enormous responsibility for sustaining a person's life? Their selfless commitment and patience was mind-boggling. I was awed. I had new respect for the title "nurse." My attitude and understanding continued to change and my trust deepened.

I thought more about dying. Finally, supremely aware of the gravity of my condition, I was attentive to every moment. It was crystal clear that however many minutes were left, each was very important. I savored each luscious breath. It was delicious. Whatever the moment brought me, pain or pleasure, I shared it inwardly in silent gratitude with my Spiritual Beloved, pure bliss.

Present moment, only moment, Radhey Radhey Radhey

("I feel so grateful to know you, even a little, dear Lord.")

Present moment, only moment, Radhey Radhey Radhey.

("How I love you, oh how I love, it hurts so good in my heart.")

Present moment, only moment, Radhey Radhey Radhey.

I smiled. What a drama this life. From time to time the respiratory therapist came by and I was able to take large hits of concentrated oxygen into my lungs. When I was able to focus, I kept my mind inward, in remembrance of God's name, God's Divine form. I imagined her sitting on a chair in my room with me with her beautiful smile and loving eyes gazing at me. After four days the worst of the tests were done. Now we had to wait for the results to be assessed and proceed with less invasive protocols. The staff established a treatment plan of drugs, and I was moved from ICU to the 7th floor, which consisted primarily of transplant patients. All were kidney and liver transplants, either post-surgery or in for treatment. The good news was that I had fewer tubes in me and they did not wake me every six hours round the clock for heart pressure tests and measures. I could sleep more comfortably and was able to get up out of bed after being flat on my back for four days. Also it wasn't quite as noisy. Over the next two weeks the flurry of unending procedures continued with echocardiograms, EKGs, and innumerable blood draws for lab tests. Blood draws every morning and evening, morning and evening, morning and evening. I would jokingly beg them to leave a little for me. How could they possibly need that much? How could there possibly be that much left?

Meantime, behind the scenes my sister was orchestrating a choreography of support from New York via email and phone calls. My utter dependency required a crew of volunteers to deliver mail, handle my household and business affairs as well as provide lots of physical and emotional support.

LAURA'S NEW HEART — I'm Alive, It's a Good Day

From: mf@hotmail
Date: Monday January 08, 2001 7:07am
To: Mary@rr.com
Subject: Letter to Laura

Mary,

Please pick up the letters to bring to Laura whenever you have time. Also, please respect Laura's wishes and do not ask to see her while you are there unless she has specifically requested to see you. These visits are extremely tiring and trying for her. It is not that she does not wish to see her friends; it is that her body cannot cope with the strain of a visit. You will hear either from me or whoever is her day companion if she wishes you to visit or she may call you on the phone herself.

Also, the ICU really frowns on more than one visitor at a time. They were very unhappy yesterday that so many people came to visit. They have been extremely tolerant. They were ready to cancel all visiting privileges but didn't have to because Laura herself requested no visitors or phone calls (after everyone left).

You probably do not know, but she can be an excellent actor and puts up a very good face in front of all her friends, then crashes right after they leave. I spoke with her last night around dinnertime. She had not eaten and was not hungry, so I don't think she had yet tried the food you brought. I know you think that Ensure is awful stuff, but it seems the only thing she likes right now and it is keeping her alive. This is more important to her physical health than any food you could prepare. What you prepare works better for her on a psychological level than on a physical level and I am glad you are doing this because all aspects of one's health are important.

Melanie

From: Mary@rr.com
Date: Monday January 08, 2001 5:49pm
Subject: Letters to Laura

Dear Melanie,
I did not receive these emails until right now when I returned from the hospital. Laura looks GREAT today. It was so nice to see her looking like "Laura". Alex and I only stayed a few minutes and took her some home prepared food at just the time they were delivering her hospital prepared cheese sandwich and Ensure. I hope she liked what we prepared. I'll stay in touch with you.

Mary

I now received two drugs—Dobutamine and Milranol—intravenously round-the-clock. That coupled with a constant supply of oxygen kept my body functioning minimally. I was always happy to see the respiratory therapist who came several times a day to utilize the special respirator that eased my labored breathing. I had a portable IV pack that I carried like a purse, so I was able to take short walks around the 7th floor. I was overjoyed at my new freedom to meander about the floor, and do slow laps around the nurse's station for ten-minute intervals. I was on one of these solo walks at a time when it was somewhat subdued on the floor. As I passed the nurse's station, I noticed a large three-ring binder with my name on it sitting on the counter. "Well this is interesting. It has my name on it, so it certainly seems I have a right to take a look. Why had I never seen the likes of this before?" I stood at the counter and read through every page of test results and doctor's notes, many of which I didn't understand. I found Dr. Jaski's note to Dr. Guarneri especially amusing and diplomatic in response to our first meeting,

LAURA'S NEW HEART — I'm Alive, It's a Good Day

"Thank you for sending me this most unique and challenging client." I had practically bitten the poor guy's head off; it gave me a chuckle. He was very gracious about it. Now I always looked forward to Dr. Jaski's daily visits and his booming voice that resonated across the entire floor whenever he arrived, "Well hello Laura, how are you doing today?"

Interesting to reflect on a 'notebook' that was kept about me, to realize I was a topic for discussion in so many places.

In between tests, exams, changing of IVs and small bursts of exercise I tried to rest. Simple conversation grew increasingly difficult, phone calls were especially depleting. I wanted desperately to be able to communicate what I was going through with someone, but it took too much breath energy. No one really seemed to get it anyway. How could they? And I wouldn't have wished this experiential understanding on anyone. Visiting friends would screen my calls. I learned to deeply enjoy silence and I listened. I heard how much gabby unnecessary nonsense we all engage in. How meaningless it seemed to me now. It was like watching bubbling waves on top of the ocean—a lot of superficial drama that meant nothing. My vision opened. It seemed as though I was looking deep inside each person that came into my room. I was connected to a quiet still part inside myself. I felt myself watching a movie with the sound turned down, as though I was in another room observing a drama. Oddly, my name kept popping up as a distant theme, but it was as though I wasn't there. It was a fascinating and noisy show with each human being separated from the deepest core of their being. This core was layered over with a personality that seemed determined not to sit still long enough to feel its own hungry need for eternal and unconditional love.

LAURA L. FINE

From: mf@hotmail
Date: Tuesday January 09, 2001 8:14am
To: BCC
Subject: Laura update

Dear friends,

Laura is somewhat more stabilized. Today she is feeling better and speaking better as well. However, I constantly have to keep in mind that "better" is all relative. She is still in cardiac ICU and will be there for awhile. What that really means is that her feeling 'better' is sometimes only a matter of an hour. But every hour is a precious one.

She has consented to have a VAD (Ventricular Assist Device) put in if it becomes necessary. This is a sort of pump that helps the heart to pump and is a temporary measure used while waiting for a new heart. Basically, it means if she goes into cardiac arrest and would otherwise die, they will put this in. It is a major surgery, but will mean an immediate improvement in her condition. The reason it is not done sooner is because of the extent of the surgery and that it is not a permanent thing. They'd rather not do two surgeries.

Laura has requested that no one visit her unless she specifically requests it. She has asked the same for phone calls. PLEASE!!! Respect these wishes. It is very difficult and exhausting to have visitors or speak on the phone. She may sound/look good while you are there, but then is completely exhausted immediately afterward. Her body needs all its strength to maintain simply staying alive. For those of you who are bringing her food or other things, please just leave them at the nurse's station and don't ask to visit.

She won't be alone, as I have arranged for one person to be her companion through the day. This person will get in touch with anyone Laura wishes to see or hear from and help arrange a visit or phone call as well as bring her all her regular mail and email.

If you are available to be a day-long companion for Laura, please let me know and I will add you to my list. So far, I have someone scheduled through around Jan 25.

For those of you new to this list, welcome! It keeps on growing!

Melanie

About this time, I began to notice the visceral sensation of the drugs keeping my physical body alive. I felt the kinesthetic sensation of my body dying. This was interesting, this was new. There were days I wanted to be out of this body. I told my sister that if I died soon, it would not be a tragedy. I had endured so much physical pain and discomfort that I didn't mind that my body would die. I didn't feel sad about it, just oddly detached. I was, however, terrified of a horrible, torturously slow and painful death.

Breathe in love, breathe out fear.

("Present moment, only moment. Stay in the moment Laura, stay in the moment. Don't look ahead.")

Breathe in love, breathe out fear.

("Right now, I'm okay, everything is okay, everything is okay. Right now in this moment, I'm okay.")

Breathe in love, breathe out fear.

("I'm still alive, the pain is not bad, it's bearable.")

I can manage one moment at a time, one breath at a time, one minute at a time.

And if I didn't die? I pondered what might happen next. I was too weak to care for myself. How would I live? Who could take on the burden of caring for me? What would happen when my money ran out? How would I endure the physical pain? Then I recognized I might not live long enough for any of these things to be a problem. I turned my attention to savoring each moment. As awareness of my failing physical systems grew, my mental consciousness became increasingly present.

I prayed. More trust was required, more surrender more faith—faith that grew and grew. And always, what followed was more peace. I learned that physical pain lessened if I didn't fight it. I used it as a prayer to my Divine Beloved. I found pleasure in simple things and tried not to think ahead or get caught up in the "what if's" of even the very near future. There were moments when peace would wash over me. I could feel the presence of my Beloved walking with me through every thought, every process, every poke of another needle, every invasive test, every blood pressure check. I remembered my teacher's precious words, "...this is good for my soul, this is good for my soul, this is good for my soul..." I repeated this over and over in my mind. It was my primary mantra, my base note. It was the hub of my central core. These words provided a context from which all experiences—pain and pleasure—could emanate. It was consoling.

Attachment to my body continued to fade. I had been so fearful of the judgements of my students and friends. Now I no longer cared. The reality of death was so close that the unreality of pride and vanity was simply wasted energy.

LAURA'S NEW HEART — I'm Alive, It's a Good Day

From: mf@hotmail.com
Date: Wednesday January 11, 2001 8:14am
To: BCC
Subject: Friends of Laura

Dear Friends,

Laura is feeling better yesterday and today. Her spirits are up. She got a nice sponge bath and washed her hair (this is a BIG DEAL in the ICU!!). She met with the head dietician of the hospital and now has many more options for her meals. She can request anything that she wants (although she still prefers the homemade food and who wouldn't!).

The Swann-Ganz catheter was removed yesterday. She was relieved because it was bothering her. This is great, because it also means that they do not need to monitor her as closely— that her condition is more stable. It may also mean she can be moved out of ICU, but no word on that yet.

For those of you wishing to improve your medical vocabulary: Swann-Ganz catheters: These are catheters placed into the pulmonary artery which carries blood from the heart to the lungs to be oxygenated. A Swann-Ganz catheter has an inflatable balloon near its tip. The catheter is capable of measuring a number of clinical variables including pulmonary wedge pressure and cardiac output.

The transplant team meets Thursday morning to make the official decision regarding putting her formally on the transplant list. So far, all tests but one (that I know of) have been completed. An antibody/antigen test has not been done/completed yet (this determines whether her normal antibody state would cause rejection of the donor tissue).

Laura requests that you now pass on whatever information you feel appropriate to anyone you wish.

Keep those cards and letters coming! She is enjoying all.

Melanie

At night I took a sleeping pill to sleep through the chaos of hospital activity. I was tired all the time and it was difficult to rest there. Always so much noise. A woman down the hall cried aloud for two days almost constantly, "Someone help me, someone help me." After the third day of listening to her moans, I stopped by her room on one of my brief walks and held her hand for a minute. She quieted momentarily, looked me in the eyes, then turned her head away and resumed pleading, "Someone help me." She was helpless, and I was helpless to help her, and I was helpless. But I felt calm in feeling helpless. She did not. I felt calm, resigned and grateful. I was graced with such serenity concerning my own helplessness—finally.

At night, I'd drift off to sleep praying, thinking of God, silently chanting His name, wondering if I would live through the night. Each morning it was a delicious moment of surprise to wake up! Then I'd realize, "Oh, I'm alive! Today is a good day, I'm still alive!" Then I'd smile in silent conversation with my Spiritual Master. He knew. On these days I would wake up and feel happy, "I feel happy today!" Then I would think, "Are you nuts? You have two IV drips in your arm, oxygen up your nose, your back is in excruciating pain, the pic line is infected and you feel happy?!" But I did, and I would laugh out loud in joy and amusement, pure grace from my Divine Spiritual Beloved.

After two weeks of intensive tests, the calculations were complete and the results were delivered to the transplant team. The team consisted of a cardiologist, two cardiovascular surgeons, an infectious disease doctor, pulmonary doctor, gastrointestinal doctor, dietician, and social worker. A world-class team of physicians assembled to put the puzzle pieces together and prepare a protocol of treatment. My name was on Thursday's weekly meeting menu. Is Laura Fine vital enough for heart transplant? Seemed odd, all these people meeting to discuss me and I wasn't invited. More talk about me without me there. I didn't care anymore. I was glad. I'll do whatever they tell me. Thursday I anxiously watched the clock, waiting for my transplant doctor to bring me the report. It was shortly after 2 p.m. when Dr. Jaski boomed into the room to deliver their assessment.

"Laura, you are a viable candidate with acceptable receptivity for a heart transplant. You meet the qualifications for a rating of 1B on the national heart transplant list. A rating of 1A means you must be in a critical care unit. We discussed installing a pacemaker and sending you home to wait for a heart, but the team feels you would not survive the surgery. You're too weak. We feel the best thing for you is to remain in the hospital until you get a heart."

I was enormously grateful for his directness and honesty. The news brought tears of both shock and reassurance at the acknowledgment and clear perspective of the ever-growing reality of my deteriorated condition. I would not be going home. I may never go home. And now, at this very moment, I am now on the national wait list for a heart transplant with a 1B rating. There was a tremendous relief that I could stay and be cared for in the hospital. I hadn't known that remaining in the hospital could be an option. I didn't have to uproot myself and try to survive a trip across the country to my sister's home or to my friends Jessica and Steve, or hire some stranger to care for me at home.

"Thank you Dr. Jaski; it feels like the right thing."

I looked around at my sweet little hospital room and called it home. Could be months. I knew just what pictures I wanted hung on the walls. I was happy with the decision. I felt safe. It would be less stressful to try to survive here. I felt I could mentally relax my hyper-vigilance, more fully surrender to my state of utter dependency and I wondered if this little hospital room was the place I would die.

I took daily trips to the hospital roof in a wheelchair escorted by a nurse's assistant or visiting friend. I drank the fresh air like manna from heaven. I savored the preciousness of life, minute by minute. I felt a growing compassion open in my heart. I was so weak; all that was left was my mind and my heart. From my newly contained environment, I looked at the world with different eyes—with an intrigued curiosity. I saw suffering all around me, fear in the eyes of patients, care and anxiety in the doctors and nurses as they hurried in and out. Their faces were transparent and I could see through to their underlying motivations. I was on 33-1/3 rpm, the world was moving at 78 rpm, or DSL speed. I observed with detachment the self-created anxiety over things beyond our control as medical professionals worked tirelessly to prevent an inevitable outcome, whatever that might be.

One morning a nurse came in and informed me of another blood draw she was going to do.

"Why? They just took my blood two hours ago. What is it for now and who ordered it?" I inquired. She got extremely huffy and gave me a generic answer.

"Whoever was on call."

"That's not good enough. You cannot touch me until I know more."

She stormed out, only to return a half-hour later, still in a snit— again prepared to take my blood.

"I found the doctor's order but the writing is illegible, we can't tell who ordered it."

"That's not good enough. Find out."

It amazed me how disconnected and desensitized some people could become to those around them. I felt as though she envied me. I was just lying there; she was running around working up a sweat. But it was my arm being jabbed for the hundredth time that day, not hers.

LAURA'S NEW HEART — I'm Alive, It's a Good Day

"I have to take your blood now," she declared in her aggravated tone. "Get the charge nurse," I commanded.

When the charge nurse arrived, I told her "I am firing my nurse, do not let her come near me again. I never want this nurse in my room again." By now I was near tears. "I want to know who ordered this test and what it's for. Why is that too much to ask?"

In my weakened state I could not allow myself to be victim to her hostility while jabbing a needle into my arm. I would not allow myself to be a captive of her need to release what I believed to be an aggressive impulse. Later I regretted my reaction. I hurt her feelings. I caused someone else pain and that did not feel good. Moreover, if I earned a reputation as a problem patient, word would get around and they wouldn't care for me. I recognized how my reactionary behavior hurt me. It was a tricky balance of hyper-vigilance and psychology in a new game of survival. It was an exhausting game to play and I felt trapped inside it.

There was a constant fluctuation of staff and personnel attending to my care—another reason I could never relax my attention. Why didn't they assign the same nurses to the same people? That would have been so much more humane, instead of this cold and constant revolving door of positive and negative staff that changed every twelve hours. Each new person had to study my chart, learn my vast array of medications, and try not to make any mistakes! The dynamic presence of each individual greatly impacted my fragile condition. I played my role on the stage of this drama, constantly observing my reactions and interactions from an increasingly neutral perspective. I let go. It wasn't apathy or fatalism; it was trust and surrender to God. It was love.

There were other nurses for whom work seemed an opportunity to repay a kindness or debt. One nurse's assistant came daily to ride me in a wheelchair up to the roof for fresh air, take me on walks around the hospital, or just check on my well-being. Her kindness and compassion were deeply nourishing. Predominantly the staff was tireless and dedicated.

I was comforted knowing nurses were just the press of a button away. I puttered around the little room that was now home. One evening in a private moment I got up to use the bathroom. I looked with curiosity at my reflection in the mirror. Who was this stranger? I felt detached from my body. This emaciated figure, the gaunt eyes, the ashen complexion were decidedly not who *"I"* was. I looked at the body in the mirror and thought, "Oh, that poor thing, that poor, poor thing. Just look at her." It was as though I was referring to someone else. But who was *she?* My body sort of tagged along with my consciousness. I began to experience that *"I"* am *not* my body. My body simply became a convenient vehicle to escort my soul, mind and consciousness from place to place on this material plane. "Poor thing." *"I,"* however, did not feel poor. There was no more resistance to my fate, no more battles, simply acceptance of the process and the unknown outcome. I trusted the truth of the teachings of my Spiritual Master and found reassurance in remembrance of him.

My consciousness is free and unrestricted by the physical boundaries of my body.

("I don't care for this thing, this borrowed body.")

My consciousness is free and unrestricted by the physical boundaries of my body.

("So odd this thing that travels along with me.")

My consciousness is free and unrestricted by the physical boundaries of my body.

(Who are your really?")

LAURA'S NEW HEART — I'm Alive, It's a Good Day

Cards arrived via hospital mail. Friends delivered home-cooked vegetarian meals that I tried to force myself to eat. Nothing tasted good anymore. Eating was now simply a necessary task to sustain life. Stacey sent me a daily comic with lovely distracting stories of her own life. Craig and Sara brought bags of healthy snacks and juices. People I hadn't heard from in years called out of the blue. It was odd. Did someone die?

My friend Jessica flew in from Cincinnati to help me. She stayed in my home, cleaned my house top to bottom, brought me clean clothes, and started to organize my residency in the hospital. I adjusted to my new hospital life-style. I gave my sister my email password and she picked up my emails in New York. Then she would forward them to my downstairs housemate, who printed them out and left them upstairs for Jessica. Jessica delivered them to me daily in the hospital— an elaborate process, but a communication link that elevated my spirit with an outpouring of love and support from friends and family. Phone calls were too laborious. I didn't have the breath to talk. I could read these letters whenever I had opportunity to rest between procedures.

One day, I received a sudden deluge of emails from former students. Apparently the word was out. A particular student had taken it upon herself to share the news of my condition with a huge email list of former students.

My reaction was mixed. I was utterly surprised when students with whom I had little contact wrote to express their concern and gratitude in vivid expressions of love. I was happy to know that they had benefited from their time with me, but I felt insignificant and believed that in actuality I had little to do with their personal achievements. I was pleased to have their remembrance and affection, but at the same time I felt oddly detached.

And I was horrified. How dare this woman share something so deeply personal, so intimate, so private with so many others without asking my permission in advance? If she were so concerned about my well-being, why didn't she contact me directly? I was in the hospital. I wasn't dead. I still had a mind, a voice, a functioning life. In her email she had asked everyone to pray for me. What if I didn't want unsolicited prayers?! If someone wanted to do something for me, didn't I have a say in it? Is it giving when we give what we want to give, even if it is not what the recipient wants to receive? I imagined my former students thinking of me with fear and pity. I was sure I was now the butt of the latest gossip for hundreds of students and colleagues. I had a hard time believing they truly cared about me. I was defensively sure that those who truly cared had already known of my condition because they were involved in my life. These were people I hadn't seen nor had contact with in years. I was utterly furious.

I was sure a litany of judgments, negative gossip, distorted self-proclaimed triumphs of psychic readings and healings were all happening on my behalf. I was told by more than one, "Oh, you really have to choose whether you want to live or die."

What kind of idiotic thinking is that! Put almost anyone face to face with death and I bet you find no one really wants to die! They just want to be OUT of pain, they don't want to be dead! As if it were in my hands! I felt such effrontery, such rage that I came face to face yet again with *my own* arrogance, pride and vanity.

I imagined others thinking of me with unspoken fear—those who needed me on an idealistic pedestal. "If Laura, my example of a nonsmoking, non-drinking, meditating, altruistic do-gooder, energy healer and health nut, could have something like this happen to her, anything could happen to me!" This only to be followed by a second, more stark thought, "No matter how many "right" things we do, we cannot control the outcome of our destiny; something horrible could happen to me, too."

LAURA'S NEW HEART — I'm Alive, It's a Good Day

These machinations of my mind stewed for days and then I got the proof I was waiting for. One student actually had the audacity to email me directly to inquire whether or not I had any insights as to *why I created something like this thing for myself?* Had she learned nothing? Now we are blaming the—and I DEPLORE the use of the word—victim! Victim! I refused to go through these circumstances as a victim. "What kind of karma did Laura secretly do that she is now paying for?" They wanted "in" to my mind and my soul, so they could find a way to escape the imagined horrors of their own karmic destiny.

I finally had a reason, a rationalization, a justification to be angry! And I was glad. The truth of the matter was that I just didn't want to be sick and I finally had someone I could be mad at. I was mad and glad that I was mad. I couldn't be mad at the doctors; they were trying their best to save me. I was sure I had to secretly "act" nice, manipulate everyone to like me so they would continue to extend themselves to help me survive. And I was scared, scared that if I got mad at my doctors or nurses, they would not do their best for me. If I became another number, another statistic, another pathetic hospital patient, they would surely lose interest in me. My insecurity and hidden layers of low self-esteem, low self-worth that I thought I had conquered, were alive, well and blaring fully in my face. I saw how little I trusted in the basic goodness of human beings. I saw my hypocrisy. I recognized how much of my behavior and even my kindness was selfishly motivated. Get them to like me, charm them so they'll care about me. *Then* they'll take good care of me. If they don't like me, they won't take care of me. I recognized this covert and shallow part of myself rising up into conscious awareness. It was startling and humiliating. It was painful.

I couldn't be mad at my friends and family. I needed them and they were offering me too much kindness and support. I couldn't be mad at the nurses or lab techs; interactions with them were too short lived and impersonal to be gratifying enough to warrant anger. I just wanted to be mad. I needed a venue for all this frustration at not being able to live my life and function the way that I wanted. I was having a full-blown temper tantrum. What was even more frustrating was that I knew it! I recognized it! Here it was, finally—the *anger* stage. I was especially furious about that—to be following the *textbook stages of crisis*. I didn't want to be in a textbook stage. I wanted to be unique. I wanted to be spiritually superior and above all that. Actually, no. What it boiled down to was I just didn't want to be sick at all, no matter how many spiritual payoffs I might gain. The worst and the best part were that I *knew* what was happening. I could not hide from myself. This became another test of surrender.

I didn't want to be mad at God. I was determined to use this anger to grow closer to Him. It took time. I stewed and fumed for several days. It felt good to be angry, it strengthened my will.

Outwardly, I complained to Jessica. We discussed the students. She too had been a student in my classes. She was familiar with the dynamics and beliefs of 'students'. Jessica helped me recognize my hidden fears and distorted perspectives. At the time I could not fully embody my anger. My body was too weak. It erupted in an ugly snippy fashion like a harmless, yet hysterical barking chijhuajua. I just didn't possess enough energy to be truly mad or even to cry. Nor did I want to. It all seemed such a ridiculous waste of time. After a few days the feelings subsided and forgiveness crept in. I reached a plateau of calm and acceptance. I did not want to die mad.

I lay in bed thinking and reviewing my life. Was there, in fact, something so terrible that I had done to create and deserve this? What had I done? What crimes, what sins? Was it that affair I had with a married man, the lies I had told? I detested this way of thinking but I forced myself to go there, to take a hard scouring look. I searched my soul, my actions and behaviors and choices in this life. Yes, I had done many things I regretted, bad actions, things I felt truly sorry for, things I would do differently if I had a chance, but nothing added up to this kind of consequence, at least in *MY* opinion. I prayed to make amends to all persons I had harmed, and did so directly whenever I could. I was probably going to die soon, I wanted to go with my conscience as clean as I could. I wanted my mind to be free and clear, to think only lovingly of God and others. I realized my students felt helpless and were seeking to lovingly support me in whatever way they could. With this understanding came forgiveness.

I believed my Spiritual Master's teachings—that I had done uncountable karmas in uncountable lives and this was simply the reaping of one of those karmas. I looked for a connection through past-life memories, and concluded that was a waste of time. I just wanted to focus my mind on devotion, to think of the Divine plays of God, to have one more precious present moment to be in love with Him. The past was over, gone. I couldn't erase it. I couldn't undo it. I could only wholeheartedly embrace each moment now.

My goal now was to prepare for the heart transplant procedure. The possibility of actually having a heart transplant still seemed foreign— so strange. My sister helped me complete a legal will. I opted for no extreme lifesaving measures. If the opportunity to die suddenly occurred in the form of ventricular tachycardia, or heart failure, it would be merciful. We all have a scheduled date with death, the only difference between me and the rest of the world was that I was spending a whole lot more time thinking about it.

I settled into the daily routine of hospital life. One would think there isn't much to do—confined to a hospital room all day—but I was kept busy with blood pressure checks, vital signs checks, blood draws at 6 a.m. and midnight. The IV packs of Dobutamine and Milranol would last five or six hours and then had to be refilled no matter what time of day or night. The nurse's assistant would check my weight at 6 a.m.; another attendant came in at 4 a.m. to refill my water. How could anyone sleep and get well?

The nursing staff changed shifts at 7 a.m. and 7 p.m. With each new shift and each new nurse, we would scope one another out. Is he/she going to be kind, adept, give me difficulty? My sister arranged for several "primary care" nurses. The charge nurse and I discussed who I would like assigned to my room whenever they were on duty. This allowed me to develop more personal relationships with some of the nursing staff. I began to feel more at home. Visits from the transplant team members could happen any time throughout the day or night. I kept a list of questions prepared for whenever they might show up, perhaps tired and haggard from an arduous surgical procedure. They observed me daily with varying degrees of consternation, and I would observe them daily with varying degrees of consternation as well. I grew to love them all.

I asked Joan, my transplant coordinator, if she could arrange for me to meet someone who had received a heart transplant. If I did survive, I might as well learn what life would be like with a heart transplant. The next day a woman came peering into my room. She looked about my age and physical size. She was very forthcoming and happy to answer all of my questions. I even asked if I could see her scar. It was scarcely noticeable. I was surprised. I was expecting it to look hideous. She was about four years out of her transplant and certainly seemed to be physically healthy but also very depressed. I felt a deep underlying disturbance as she rattled off a list of her medications that included antidepressants. It was unsettling. Was I going to turn out like this?

I scheduled a meeting for Joan and Rauni, the healing touch nurse, the following week. My plan was to have Joan talk me through the surgical procedure. I wanted to know what happened in complete detail from start to finish. Then Rauni would guide me through the same process once more, this time under hypnosis so I could prepare my body to be receptive to the experience—whenever it might come. I believed the hypnosis would facilitate my body's natural healing mechanism and encourage compatibility with the new heart after the surgery—if I could hang on long enough and was fortunate enough to receive a donor heart.

The next day, two more heart transplant recipients dropped by. It was around eleven in the morning when a woman in her sixties stepped in with her husband. She explained that she had just been in for her semiannual biopsy. She was wearing a mask, as instructed by the transplant doctor. "Because of the immune suppressants recipients must take after their transplants, they are at greater risk for infection when they are in hospital environments," she explained. Joan reassured me that hospitals were the only place that especially required that precaution. This woman had her new heart for about five years. I liked her immediately.

She was warm, friendly, happy and grateful. Somehow this procedure, while limiting her activity to some degree, had not really interfered with her joy of life. I felt comforted. That same afternoon, another woman stopped by. In her late fifties, she too was very upbeat and warm, with a buoyant personality and quick mind. She answered many questions and offered a great deal of empathy and understanding about my situation and condition. After she left, I felt relief and a greater sense of hope. But I still wasn't entirely convinced that I would live a normal life. There were a great deal of physical limitations, it seemed, and each person's outcome was so unique. How would it go for me? Would it go for me? Would I live long enough to even have the opportunity to get a heart?

Nights in the hospital were still an adjustment. It seemed the only way to sleep through the constant commotion of hospital living was to continually succumb to sleeping pills. Even with the constant flurry, I liked nights in the hospital. Most of the time the pace was slower and more peaceful. My little window looked out onto the heliport. Many evenings deep into the night I would hear the whirrrr of the chopper arrive on its landing. When I couldn't sleep I would get up, go to the window and watch in the quiet as the ER team would unload some mangled soul from the stretcher. It was not a fun day for that person. It had not yet occurred to me that the body on that stretcher might contain a heart for me.

It was reassuring to know that I could call a nurse anytime. Terry was one of my favorites. She was compassionate and caring. I was happy whenever she was on a night shift with me. She would always take a moment to sit on my bed, ask about my day, give me a hug, and tuck me in. I welcomed her warm mothering energy and felt especially nurtured when she was on board. In the quiet of the hospital night I would reflect on my life, on the fact that I was still alive, could still think, could still love, could still remember God, my Spiritual Master, family and friends. It required much effort to reach my tape player to listen to my chanting meditation tapes. Most of the time it was all I could do to just use my mind to remember…remember…and with the help of the sleeping pill, I drifted off to sleep with a prayer that I wake up for one more blessed morning.

LAURA'S NEW HEART — I'm Alive, It's a Good Day

Locked inside my being are depths of passion and courage that have lived untapped, unnoticed by my mind. As I drop into my core, I command this strength to rise up to my consciousness now.

My core makes known my formerly unknown strengths which are ...

_____

_____

_____

_____

_____

_____

_____

_____

_____

_____

_____

_____

The images above are an invitation to self-reflect, explore and discover more of the depths of your soul's mysterious beauty. You may wish to utilize the space above to respond to the image, designed to stimulate your creative subconscious mind. Taking a few minutes to journal your response to the thought, invites an opportunity to deepen your contact with your loving spiritual nature.

LAURA L. FINE

Chapter Six: *Laura's New Heart*

I counted backwards. I had been at Scripps Hospital for three weeks. I was transferred to Sharp Hospital two weeks ago upon agreement to test for viable heart transplant candidacy. I had spent the past two weeks filled with angiograms, pic lines, daily blood tests, echocardiograms, x-rays. Three days had passed since the tests were completed and Dr. Jaski had told me I was approved and on the list for heart transplantation. It was 10:30 p.m. on the third day after being put on the 'waiting list' when Terri, my favorite primary care night nurse, came into my room.

"Laura, you're about to get a phone call." I got nervous. It was late. No nurse had ever come into my room and informed me in advance of a phone call. She sat down next to me on the bed. Obviously, something was up. I couldn't imagine what had happened. The seconds ticked by. I glanced tensely at the phone just as it yelled a loud ring. When I picked up the phone, Joan, the transplant team coordinator was on the line. I'll never forget her words.

"Laura, I think we have a heart for you. We'll know for sure in about an hour. Dr. Adamson has to see it first. He looks it over to make sure it's not bruised or damaged."

"*Oh my God, oh my God, oh my God,*" was all I could repeat, over and over again. I started shaking like a leaf. I was terrified and thrilled at the same time.

"If the heart is good, surgery will begin at 2 a.m. She paused. "Do you want to do this?"

"YES!... NO!... YES! *I don't know. How can I not? It's so soon, it's just so soon!*" I couldn't wrap my brain around this news.

My hands were shaking as I dialed my sister and woke her up. It was

2 a.m. in New York. I was hyperventilating. Although she tried hard to calm me down, I could not slow my breathing. I paged Dr. Guarneri. She called back in less than five minutes. With my voice trembling and my breath hyperventilating, I was in a full-scale panic attack. I managed to get my voice out...

"Dr. Guarneri, they have a heart for me."

She had just finished a business dinner and as it so happened was with Rauni, who had come to the hospital two days previously and had done a healing touch session on me. Just as she was leaving after the session, Rauni paused in the doorway and casually remarked, "You know, just in case a heart should come in before I see you next week, you know you can page Dr. Guarneri. She will know how to reach me." I didn't think much about her comment. I figured this sweet little hospital room would be home for many months to come. I couldn't comprehend this procedure actually occurring. It was too surreal.

"Rauni and I will be right there," Dr. Guarneri said.

The next call I made was to one of my spiritual sisters. I asked her to come and be with me. Then I called my house and told Jessica. My devotee friends Mary and Alex, Dr. Guarneri, Rauni, and Jessica all arrived at the hospital within twenty minutes.

Rauni began a healing touch/hypnotherapy treatment. I fell under with tremendous receptivity. It was as though my entire being was falling into a well of "*Yes, Yes, Yes.*" I was a starving person, being fed manna from heaven under her words, suggestions and energy.

"You are walking down a slope toward a beautiful beach...it is peaceful there, you are becoming more and more deeply relaxed as you go, your body is relaxing..." I surrendered everything in my being. I gave over entirely to her voice, her words and energy. I let go on levels I didn't know possible and felt myself falling into the presence of my Divine Beloved.

There was no other recourse now, just to trust. It was as though I were standing in front of a gigantic roller coaster with a ticket in my hand, dressed in my pajamas. No time to think or question, just get on for the ride. It was a first. I have always hated roller coasters. But this time, I mounted the ride, I let go and let myself be carried.

"As they bring you into the operating room, your body feels completely relaxed, safe and receptive. The cells of your body know what is going to happen and they feel calm and happy. This new heart will live peacefully and happily in the home of your body…your body will receive it joyfully and they will work in harmony together…"

In less than three minutes, my breathing slowed dramatically. I trusted Rauni and began to feel safe, calm, happy and at ease as I clung for dear life to her soothing words. She guided me with her loving voice and the energy healing touch of her hands and in thirty minutes, I felt sleepy and giddy with a relaxed excitement. There was no fear anywhere in my body or mind. I had taken no tranquilizers. I simply surrendered. The transition was startling.

When Mimi and Rauni left, a delicious calm permeated the room. Mary, Alex and Jessica sang beautiful devotional chants and I was washed in the sweetness of God's love. Two a.m. came quickly. I was still deeply calm and happy when Mary and Jessica accompanied me as my gurney headed for the operating room. Rolling along the silent hallway I wondered if I would ever wake up again. I felt peaceful. If today was to be my time of death, it's okay. My thoughts drifted calmly and I chuckled in a quiet and present state of calm.

"…there's a Special
Providence in the fall of a sparrow. If it be now, 'tis not
to come: if it be not to come, it will bee now : if it

be not now; yet it will come; the readiness is all, since no
man has ought of what he leaves. What is't to leave betimes?"

Hamlet, V.2

I felt ready for whatever was to come. I told my sister on the phone that if I died it would not be a tragedy. I was happy with my life. I felt the closeness of my Divine Beloved walking beside me along the hallway to the operating room. I said to Mary, "I know that He knows it is happening now." The anesthesiologist came out to meet me and wheeled me into the surgery room. We had an informative conversation. Even in my relaxed state, I was ever instructing.

"Now, I have this little bird body, so please keep that in mind..." It didn't take long to again let go and recognize that he was very present, an expert in his field. I chuckled at myself, at the inanity of my controlling nature even in this situation—ever instructing, ever the teacher. I let go and relaxed. Looking around at all the odd technology, I felt no fear. I had surrendered and it was comforting. I closed my eyes, lying on the cold table, and felt the presence of God hovering in the upper right corner of the operating room, smiling sweetly down at me.

"Now crackes a Noble heart:
Goodnight sweet Prince,
And flights of Angels sing thee to thy rest,..."

Hamlet, Act V.ii

I was ready now. If I don't wake up here, wherever I wake up it will be okay.

The surgery took about five to six hours. I learned later from Jessica that during the procedure she sat up all night in the hospital lobby keeping vigil, pacing, dozing and announcing to strangers at random, "My friend is getting a heart transplant, right now. Can you believe it?"

It was about 7 a.m. when Jessica learned I was out of surgery, that it went well and I was in ICU in recovery. She drove to the airport to pick up our friend Judy. We three, Jessica, Judy and Laura had been the dearest of sister like friends for over fifteen years. For over a month Jessica had pre-planned her trip to come and help take care of me, and Judy planned to overlap her scheduled week with Jessica so that the three of us could enjoy some time together. We were amazed that unbeknownst to any of us, their arrivals would coincide at the exact time of my receiving a heart! Coincidence? Impossible! How detailed is the graciousness of this choreography, as if there weren't already an enormity of details to appreciate. How humbled can one become? Who can define good or bad anymore? My new job was about becoming receptive to everything, not questioning anything. When Jessica arrived at the airport to pick up Judy, they took a drive to the bay in the early morning quiet. Judy as yet had no idea that from the time she departed in her travel from the East Coast to the West Coast, I'd received a heart. They sat together by the water and screamed and wept in joy, relief and amazement at the events and the timing of a dance beyond comprehension.

When I awoke in ICU, Joan was sitting at by my bedside along with Bridget, the ICU nurse and maybe someone else, I can't recall. I pointed to my heart with hand signals. The first question in my mind was, "Did it work?" After all, I had been *out*. For all I knew, they could have installed one of those mechanical heart pumps in me. She beamed her inspiring smile and seemed to understand.

"Yes," she said, "you have a new heart. You're doing really well!"

I felt relieved and fell back to sleep.

The next time I awoke I saw the face of my dear sister sitting beside me. I was so happy and comforted to see her. I was amazed how quickly she had gotten from New York to San Diego – I didn't realize I had lost all sense of time during the surgery. A breathing tube was stuffed down my throat, but the two other transplant survivors I had met had warned me that "the breathing tube is the worst part." So I felt prepared and actually thought, "Well gee, it's really not that bad."

No, the worst part was an incredible thirst. My mouth and throat felt so dry from the tube that I desperately wanted water. The nurse kindly explained that was not possible. Instead, she swabbed my throat with a wet washcloth. It helped. I motioned that I wanted to write. I had questions, of course. My sister understood and they got me a clipboard. I wrote my question again.

"Did it work? Do I have a heart?"

"Yes," my sister said, "You have a new heart."

"It's a miracle!" I wrote, in chicken scrawl. My vision was severely blurred and my hand shook.

"Yes," Melanie said.

Well, this was a first for me.

"When does this breathing tube come out? What can I do to help my breathing?" I scribbled.

I was informed there was nothing I could do, just wait and be patient. I think I fell back to sleep again. The breathing tube came out about five or six hours later. The doctors were very pleased that I could breathe again so quickly on my own.

My sister called her partner Dara and dictated the email to her over the phone in New York.

From: mf@hotmail.com
Date: January 18, 2001 3:06 p.m.
To: BCC
Subject: Laura's new heart

At 10 p.m. last night Laura received a phone call letting her know they had a heart for her. She went into surgery at 2 a.m. The surgery was a success and she is doing well. I saw her in ICU where she is recovering. I will keep you posted. GREAT NEWS EVERYBODY!!!

Melanie

I spent five days in ICU after the transplant, and then moved back to the 7th floor. Good. More tubes came out. Laurel, a nurse and energy healer, stopped by to offer me a session. I accepted gratefully. After a solid week of constant invasion from the surgery and follow-up procedures, I was racked with pain and tension, while emotionally I was worried that my body would reject the heart. Laurel relaxed her hands deeply into my body. I felt a profound shift in the room, in myself. We entered into a state of consciousness that carried me away. I went out, and came to when she quietly got up to leave. I had a sense something in me had shifted. I waved a soft good-bye, too exhausted to do more and for the first time in five days, I was able to drift into a deep-relaxed sleep.

I was healing quickly. Though I was tired and weak, there was a life force now present in my body. My cheeks were flushed with blood, rosy pink, a far cry from the ashen white I had worn so many months. It was as though I went through a revolving door, and when I came out the other side, there was chi in my body.

The next miracle is the CMV story. CMV is a virus that apparently lives in about 60% of the population. It is a similar strain to the herpes virus. Prior to the transplant I tested negative for CMV, but the donor heart tested positive. The transplant team was deeply concerned this incompatibility might cause rejection after the transplant. They were closely monitoring me. In my first blood test after the transplant, I tested positive for CMV! How did that happen?! Did I catch CMV from the new heart? Did Laurel's energy healing session have something to do with it? No one had an explanation. Maybe this was another first. The good news was that now our immune systems were immensely more compatible.

Once out of ICU and back on the 7th floor, I had to transition from IV anti-rejection drips to oral anti-rejection pills. This was another huge feat. "I hardly took an aspirin all my life," I explained, "let alone this stream of medication." How on earth could I do this? How would this become a part of my life? What sat before me was a tray of more than thirty pills of various shapes, sizes and colors with a matching list full of descriptions, contraindications and side effects. It took every ounce of my energy just to eat a meal, bathe myself, do my simple exercises. How on earth would I be able to adapt to this for the rest of my life? The ensuing stomach pain was horrible. I have always had a delicate digestive tract, and now I had to digest and assimilate some thirty pills a day—immune suppressants, steroids, pain pills, and sleeping pills. My years as an HHP made it difficult to wrap my mind around these new circumstances. For example, I tried to take the minimum dose of pain pills, until I realized that was absurd. I was putting thirty other medications in my body! What on earth difference did it make if I took two pain pills instead of one?! I laughed at the ridiculousness of my programmed limiting mind. After all I had been through I certainly wasn't dead yet! How much would it take to realize that no matter how 'pure' I think I am being with my body, the laws of karma are at work with their own rules. What will be will be, whether or not this matches up with my foolish beliefs about controlling the outcome of events by living in accordance with my perception of the laws of nature. Karma is simply playing itself out in my physical body, no matter how much control I let myself believe I might have in the dance. After all, now drugs were saving my life. Without the drugs my body would reject the new heart and I'd be dead! Bring on the Dr. Feelgoods!!! It was full steam ahead for the power of drugs! Forget the carrot juice, I started drinking Coke! Boy I had been craving a coke!

"Jessica, get me a coke, let's celebrate!" I haven't had a Coke in twenty years! That was almost a first! After all, what difference did a Coca-Cola make with all these drugs in my body? It was freeing!

With time, my body adjusted. I compromised my new found freedom of Coca-Cola when I learned that drinking a high protein shake with my pills and eating high-protein vegetarian foods helped me assimilate the medications. After a few days, the stomach pain eased a bit.

I reflected on the uncanny timing of events that could only have been choreographed by God. How could it be that Jessica became available for two weeks and flew in from Cincinnati just four days before I received a heart? How could it be that Judy, who had scheduled her visit weeks in advance, arrived the day of my surgery? How could it be that after trying for three weeks unsuccessfully to arrange for a home care helper, I heard that a friend was available to work for me the same day I was scheduled to arrive home from the hospital? These were only a few of the dozens of uncanny scenarios that occurred during those months. I stopped discriminating between what seemed "good" and what seemed "bad." I was filled with gratitude, awe and wonder. I felt that God was personally overseeing and orchestrating every detail of my life. I had no more room for feelings of 'false humility', only wonder at how God could be so personally aware of each detail of my needs. My faith grew, not because of the 'good things' that were happening, but because I felt His kind presence, His humor and delight—with more awareness. Perhaps it was simply me, finally paying more attention.

I could not yet look at my bandaged chest scar. I wasn't ready to see it. After about a week, they gave me my first shower and washed my hair, pure heaven. The next twelve days saw a gradual and amazing daily improvement. I cried daily, frequently, happy tears of enormous relief, grief and gratitude. I was filled with life force. I felt this beautiful new heart working, pumping precious blood throughout my body. I had color in my face. I had a voracious appetite. I had been starving for so many months and now I could eat and digest my food!

I started to walk again. I looked like an old lady, hunched and rounded, weak and trembling. My body, arms and legs had atrophied terribly from my six weeks in the hospital. Soon the nurse had me climb a flight of stairs. A wondrous achievement! I took my first shower by myself after another week and felt so proud that I announced it at the nurse's station.

"I took a shower by myself; I took a shower by myself!" I was too overjoyed to feel embarrassed. I was like a toddler just learning how to bathe and walk, with all the same proud excitement.

About eight days passed before I mustered the courage to look at my scar. I expected a grotesque black tire track on my chest. It wasn't so bad. They actually did a very impressive job. In an odd sort of way I felt kind of proud, like a warrior who had survived battle. It was my badge of conquest. Remarkably, I had triumphed. I was still alive.

My sister sent out the news via email. The subject: Laura's New Heart. A stream of responses poured in. Reactions were hugely emotional. I was the focal point of a sort of self-reflective process for many, but this time in a role not of my own making. My friend Ray used to always tease me, "Laura, wherever you are, whatever you participate in, you always seem to manage to get right up front at the center of things." Somehow the Leo in me was never shy of direct contact with the leaders or teachers at the heart of any program or organization with which I was involved. I was up front and center stage again but I felt so humbled by the magnificence of these events that I perceived these attentions as woefully misdirected and myself as undeserving.

My gratitude for life was inexpressible. The blessing, gift and miracle of this new heart was beyond my scope of appreciation or understanding. The immense humility that I felt was indescribable. My perspective about life could no longer be the same. How could I worry about the rent? God arranged a new heart for me, rent is easy!

Twelve days and two biopsies later, they released me to go home. I was terrified and happy. I was on a high dose of prednisone (steroid) along with the many other drugs, which gave me numerous side effects including the most horrific panic attacks. I could not control my emotions. Jessica ended up extending her stay a week and was now preparing to leave. Judy also extended her stay to relieve Jessica and worked hard to take care of the many necessary arrangements of my after care. Judy screened my calls, prepared my home for my return, and brought me Lotsa Pasta.

After Judy's shift came Mary, a former student, actress, comedienne and friend from L.A. Mary took me home from the hospital and helped me transition. That week was one of the most difficult of my life. Without Mary's tremendous patience, love, sense of humor, cooking, and cleaning, I don't know what I would have done. I didn't know how to recover from heart transplant surgery or what to expect.

Prednisone overwhelmed me with anxiety. The dynamic of the drug ensnared my mind in a perpetual state of panic and anxiety almost twenty-four hours a day. There was a two-hour window from about four to six p.m. when the drug would wear down enough that I felt I could peek out from under its heavy coat. In those moments I would turn to Mary and say, "Mary, it's me again, I'm back. The drug let go and I feel okay," only to have to ingest another dose and feel the horrific panic attacks resume their grip. Mary would follow my panicked fearful instructions with a cheerful lilting, "aaallll right!" It made me laugh inside every time I heard it. I couldn't laugh out-loud because my chest was still raw from the surgery, but it lifted my spirits each time. I hung on tight to prayer and distraction. After about seven days, my doctor decreased the prednisone dosage and the nightmare eased. I went to the hospital for my third biopsy, my third celebratory report of "no rejection."

Rauni and Liz continued to give me energy healing treatments. Rauni worked to harmonize the energetic cords of my new donor heart with my body. Judson came frequently to massage my traumatized body. We celebrated the birth of his son, born three days after my own rebirth.

There were manifold details needing attention in order to prepare for the next six months of recovery, and I was practically helpless to execute any of them myself. I was still so vulnerable and in the beginning stages of recovery. What would happen after Mary returned to work? I was hugely relieved when my dear cousins Kenny and Anita said they would come for twelve days and take over my care.

I began to exercise, to walk. After about a month, I was walking an hour a day and doing simple yoga and stretching exercises. After Kenny and Anita returned home, Beth and her husband gave me an extraordinary gift. A gourmet food service came to my home and did my cooking for a month! It was two months after the surgery before I could drive and manage my own cooking and cleaning. I entered Dr. Guarneri's wonderful cardiac rehab program at Scripps Hospital. Classes in yoga, exercise, stress management, group support and nutrition met three days a week for six months. I was the only heart transplant in a recovery group with a dozen others who were healing from coronary artery disease, bypass surgery and other heart related problems. I started seeing clients again part-time. New clients facing life-threatening health challenges seemed to make their way to my doorstep almost immediately. How did that happen? It was uncanny. By the end of the third month I had enough strength to cook for myself.

One of my greatest rewards came when I was able to give both Rauni and Dr. Guarneri an energy healing treatment. I longed to be able to share, to give back, to have them experience the healthy side of me. I wanted to be known as more than a weak, sickly, dependent person. It was my intrinsic human need to prove my worth and contribute something of value.

I learned that surrender, faith and trust also included letting go of how my outward contribution to the world was to be expressed, not 'my will' but thy will. In one of our rehabilitation support group processes, one of the participants said, "I'm worthless because I can't do anything; I'm too old, too weak and too sick." A mixture of emotions flooded through me. I was angry and impassioned at his comment. I responded quickly with the self-realization, "Maybe your job right now is to receive. If there were no one to be sick, then those who need to give right now wouldn't have anyone to service. Perhaps it is they, *more than you*, that are in need, need of the opportunity to heal themselves by serving another."

Today could be the very last time I ever see you alive, I ever speak to you, I ever have the pleasure and pain of knowing you.

What I want you to know that I may have never before expressed in quite this way is...

The images above are an invitation to self-reflect, explore and discover more of the depths of your soul's mysterious beauty. You may wish to utilize the space above to respond to the image, designed to stimulate your creative subconscious mind. Taking a few minutes to journal your response to the thought, invites an opportunity to deepen your contact with your loving spiritual nature.

LAURA L. FINE

Chapter Seven: *Assimilation*

Each day I pray, meditate and give thanks. I continue to be deeply grateful and pray that these feelings of gratitude never ever leave me. There has been one episode of minor level two rejection from the heart, which was easily treated with a temporary dosage increase of immune suppressant medication. Of my new heart, I feel we are happily married together, our atriums sewn one on top of the other in a loving embrace.

I have no regrets for what happened to me, only gratitude—another first. I have a new respect for western medicine, and for doctors and nurses as compassionate humanistic people who are also part of the healing profession. I respect the power and technology of modern medicine and pharmaceuticals in a way that I did not before. I'm happy to say that I am off Dobutamine, Milranol, Coumadin, Ace inhibitors, diuretics, pain pills, antidepressants, sleeping pills and my short lived celebration of Coca-Cola. I am now on a delicate balance of two immune suppressants and lots of vitamins. I still take Co-Q10 in 100 mg. tablets. I embrace all fields—western, eastern and holistic—as complimentary medicine.

The first two years out of transplant my aftercare included four heart biopsies per year to check for rejection. During the biopsies, Dr. Jaski allowed me to bring Rauni into the cardiac catheterization lab to give me energy healing therapy. I did not have to give up my holistic beliefs or practices. I merely added a new perspective, affirming the value of western medicine.

I've come to reflect upon my own denial, as one aspect of a natural survival mechanism. It enabled me to make a full commitment to every choice I made in my journey toward health.

"This above all; to thine owne self be true:
And it must follow, as the Night the Day,
Thou canst not then be false to any man."

Hamlet I.iii

What myself and others may refer to as denial I came to view with a different perspective. Perhaps denial was actually the subtle underpinnings of my karma unwinding limiting psychological beliefs that actually served me well. Perhaps that is simply rationalization for shame about having denial. In either case I learned to lessen my mental torture by repeatedly turning to my faith and consoling myself with the mantra, *"Our Divine Mother knows what is good for every soul, and she is caring for you."* It enabled me to "die while living." What died along the way were many trivial attachments. I became clear and firm about my priorities, my spiritual life, my trust and awareness in God's presence. My intensified practice of devotional remembrance of God gave me an ability for greater recognition of His presence moment to moment and an experience of overwhelming gratitude for each breath I inhale. I was surprised and awed at the outpouring of support and love from family and friends. At the same time, I often experienced an extreme feeling of loneliness and desire for increased intimacy with my beloved God and Guru.

The spiritual lessons and gifts I received have made this journey a most precious, priceless gift. I would not trade it for anything, though it has been the most challenging time of my life. *"Our Divine Mother knows what is good for every soul, and She is caring for you."* These words are still my mantra. Every day throughout this journey I have said them over and over. I continue to do so today. I pray to continue to recognize not only the "big" miracles of my heart and my life, but also the "little" miracles that occur each day. These I did not see so clearly before. Each situation, relationship, confrontation, conversation, each detail, each event, is an opportunity to experience life's gifts from God. Each challenge offers the possibility to move closer to God; the opportunity to hear each spoken word from another's mouth as "good for my soul."

On the emotional level, I am still processing. Along my journey I observed many others in life struggles. I have learned that we all go through a "heart transplant" of sorts at various times in our lives. Mine happened to be literal. I do not feel special, or that I have great virtue for surviving. Mostly I just feel happy, peaceful and grateful. This creates a softness in my being—a receptivity—and that feels good. The gifts are so deep. I can only lovingly feel the thank you for all these firsts.

About fifteen months after my surgery, I was on a plane to San Antonio to teach a workshop. I wear a mask on the plane to help protect my suppressed immune system should anyone in the cabin be ill. I explained to the man sitting next to me that I did not have SARS, nor was I was contagious, but that I had had a heart transplant. He was intrigued and asked many questions, surprised that I looked so young and healthy.

"How did it happen?" he inquired. I learned he was in his mid-forties, a wealthy businessman with a family and three young children.

"They don't know. When they don't know, they say it's a virus."

"Oh." He paused. Well do you have any ideas yourself about what may have caused it?"

"No," I explained. "I've lived a very healthy life style all my life—exercise, vegetarian diet, meditation. I'm a wholistic health practitioner," I said.

He looked stunned and agitated.

"You are every healthy person's nightmare," he said.

"I know. But it's the best thing that has ever happened to me."

He turned his head away in disbelief. He couldn't see the smile under my mask and probably wouldn't have truly believed that I meant it.

As I reflect on these experiences I try to stay conscious of the curtain of maya that keeps me in the illusion that my body's death is not impending and that I have a magical health formula to stave it off with diet, exercise, meditation, healing, yagyas and prayer. I continue to do my part, best I can to stay healthy, but the mysteries of the big picture are so beyond my comprehension that I can only bow in humility and gratitude for the feelings of love and awe. I now cling to these feelings much tighter than I cling to this physical body. I struggle to stay awake and remember as I walk in a dream like state of perpetual forgetting that each breath is one breath closer to my death. Having the gift of looking nose to nose in the face of death, I see how part of my mind frequently falls into a dreamlike state of forgetting. What pleasure are we all running toward? And when we achieve these pleasures, then what? We run toward the next greater pleasure—a concert, a vacation, a new job, a new lover. We run fast and far away from anything uncomfortable—illness, disease, old age, poverty. We do anything to avoid experiencing the sensations of helplessness, surrender and humility—feelings that inevitably follow only when *forced* upon us. Then comes the realization of our utter dependence upon God's mercy for internal peace of mind. We fight hard to keep from feeling the sensations locked away in buried questions whose answers live just a hair's breath beyond the conscious and subconscious levels of the mind—for answers that can only be glimpsed. We seek relief that can only be felt through surrender of will and mind to the cry of the heart and soul's longing for God's Divine love.

Regarding some responses to my story—many people have inquired about the donor of my heart. Who was the person? What do you know about him/her? Do you know how he/she died? Do you think your personality has changed because of the new heart? Do you find yourself doing unexplainable things? Can I tell you what I have picked up psychically about them?

"NOOOOOOO" is all I want to howl! I don't know and I don't want to know. Just as my body has been given for this lifetime, God has given this heart to me through the generosity of the donor family. I have been given another heart, not another chance. According to my belief system, heart failure, heart transplant has been part of my destiny for this lifetime. Some people continue to ask, "Do you know what your *issues* are and why you *created* this horrible illness for yourself?" Did I create this for myself? The laws of karma say "yes", but not in the way we might understand the meaning of karma. My answer to them is in alignment with Hindu scriptures. The Vedas say that we have lived uncountable lifetimes, that the soul is eternal and Divine, has always existed, was never born and can never die. The body is temporary; yet we are reborn with a body time and again until as soul, we achieve God realization. Then the soul becomes Divine and resides joyfully in the Divine abode. The Vedas say that since we have lived *uncountable* lifetimes, we have *all* committed uncountable good deeds and uncountable bad deeds. A certain portion of these karmas are destined to be fructified in each lifetime; the major events in our lives are part of this karmic destiny. For me it no longer matters why or how my illness came about. I have done uncountable good and bad actions in uncountable lifetimes. I am simply living out some of their effects in this life. I cannot avoid them, whether I run to a mountain-top to meditate at the correct energy grid or sacrifice my first born.

I did not know that I would feel grateful and happy about going through heart failure, surgery and transplant. I expected to be curious about the donor, but to my surprise I am not. I have noticed no strange food cravings, no big personality change. I don't want a beer after dinner nor do I desire to go swing dancing or have a sudden interest in racehorses. I am still me, just me. That is all I want to be, and all that I am—just myself with the same personality quirks, imperfections, and individuality.

What then has changed? Perhaps I have gained a few insights, along with a few pounds. Perhaps I have a different perspective. Each day I wake up I think to myself, "I am alive, today is a good day!" Do I still experience physical pain and discomfort? Yes, but who doesn't? Do I sometimes retreat into self-pity and fear? Sure. But most days, I feel happy, content and grateful. In fact, I have learned to be grateful even for the few rough days I still have.

I am now over two years out of my transplant. I'm working full time and see clients for counseling, healing and coaching. I have co-founded an energy healing school that has three branches throughout the United States. I completed my Master's Degree in Marriage and Family Therapy and teach wholistic healing at the UCLA hospital to heart transplant recipients. I have moved into a spiritual center to become more actively involved in my spiritual community. During my reintegration into the land of the living, I've discovered that dying is easy; it's living that is challenging. It is challenging to sustain an attitude of gratitude, to stay in remembrance of God and not be seduced by the transitory pleasures of the world.

When people I meet for the first time learn I have had a heart transplant, they sometimes regard me with an odd sort of wonder and respect. Upon reading my story, many have commented how brave I am. That is difficult for me to understand. I don't feel brave, nor did I feel brave along the way. A brave person is one who takes a risky voluntary action to help another. My actions were always motivated by survival, generated out of my limited belief patterns. I do not feel that I am special nor extraordinary. What I did and do have choice about is the attitude with which I face my challenges. I try to keep my mind positive and spiritually focused. If you find courage in my story and it is useful to you in some way, I am glad. If my story helps or inspires you in some way, then my sharing has served a beneficial purpose. My hope is that I can give back to my Beloved God some of the sweet love, mercy and kindness that have been showered upon me through His and Her Grace.

In the final edits of this book, I am now 3 years post transplant. Thanks to the wonders of classical homeopathy, I have regained my stamina. This new level of endurance has bought me freedom I never dreamt would again be possible. My souls longing to complete a dream of many many years will soon be realized. I leave next month for a trip to India to meet the Supreme Jagadguru of this age, my Spiritual Master's Master. It is not within my capability to express the gratitude and honor that I feel for this opportunity.

How I am punish'd with a sore distraction...

In the end of the play, Hamlet realized the short temporary state of life in a physical body.

Imperious Caesar, dead and turn'd to clay,
Might stop a hole to keep the wind away.
O that that earth, which kept the world in awe,
Should patch a wall t' expel the winter's flaw!

Hamlet V.i

Hamlet achieved an awakening. He realized the temporariness of the physical body, that his spirit was his essential essence. He strived to use his life's unspeakable challenges to question, seek and grow. He learned how his lack of self-control, over his passions and emotions hurt himself, hurt others. Finally willing to surrender his pride he begs forgiveness from Laertes.

> *Let my disclaiming from a purpose'd evil*
> *Free me so far in your most generous thoughts,*
> *That I have shot my arrow o'er the house,*
> *And hurt my brother.*

Hamlet, V:ii

I have hurt my Creator. I missed the magnificent beauty of His loving Grace and vibrant presence in my heart by focusing on the gifts S/he has given me through material worldly relationships and pleasures. I learned that it is my Beloved creator from whom I wish to beg forgiveness. I now dedicate my life to learning how to increasingly grow in love with the **giver** of these gifts, to live every moment in ever-increasing surrender and gratitude, that I may one day fully realize the love, mercy and kindness of God.

> *The rest is silence.*

Hamlet, V:ii

Appendix I: *Affirmations*

AFFIRMATIONS FOR PRACTICAL USE

The affirmations (or mantras) below are a compilation of inspirational thoughts gathered from numerous teachers. Their use can be most effective when you find yourself stuck in a pattern of negative thinking. Simply replace the negative thoughts with the silent repetition of one of the following affirmations. Over time you will notice the positive affects their use will have on your breathing and sense of well being.

Just for today,
I choose to accept an unacceptable situation.

Through the breath, I release my stress.

Fear = False Evidence Appearing Real

I breathe in the present moment,
I breathe out the past.

Present moment — Only moment.

I use the mind, to heal the mind.

One moment at a time lets me manage, one thought
at a time, one breath at a time, one minute at a time,
one hour at a time, one day at a time.
I can manage one day at a time.

I inhale discernment, I exhale judgment.

I breathe in life force, I release out tension.

I breathe in love, I breathe out fear.
Each breath touches my true mind,
seated in my heart center.

Each breath directs me to the
presence of love in my heart.

The present is the point of power.

Identify…instead of identify with.

Discernment eludes us when we cease
to relate to the essence of another.

I am safe, it's only change.

My cells are imbued with
loving presence of the Divine.

I breathe in love, I breathe out fear.

LAURA L. FINE

*Pain is the yellowbrick road to
my spiritual destination.*

*My consciousness is free and unlimited. It is
unrestricted by the physical boundaries of my body.*

Breathe to receive the loving presence of God.

*I wash my mind with the
breath energy of my heart.*

*Love imbues every breath, and fills
my lungs, my heart, and my mind.*

The True mind, lives in the heart center.

*I surrender my fears to the power of Love
and feel myself carried in the arms of Grace.*

I turn away from the past, I savor the present.

*Our Divine Mother knows what is good for
every soul, and she is caring for you.*

Appendix II: *Organ Donation*

I wish to acknowledge all the donors and their families for giving the most
:eless gift anyone could give to another—the gift of life.

As of September 1st, 2003, there are 82,642 people waiting to receive an
an transplant. Many will die waiting. Since 1986 approximately 65,000
·ple worldwide have received the gift of a donated heart.

HOW DO I BECOME AN ORGAN DONOR?
Decide to be an Organ & tissue donor...

re your life. Share your decision is a simple, yet important description of how
can become an organ and tissue donor. This simple two-step process will
ɔ ensure that your personal desire to become a donor will be fulfilled.

:P ONE

ANSPLANTATION is one of the most remarkable success stories in the
:ory of medicine. In most cases, it's the only hope for thousands of people
fering from organ failure, or in desperate need of corneas, skin, bone or
er tissue. Tragically, the need for donated organs and tissues continues to
:pace the supply. Right now, thousands of Americans could be helped if
)ugh organs and tissues were available. Organ and tissue donation pro-
·es each of us with a special opportunity to help others. You can save lives
making the decision to be an organ and tissue donor.

EP TWO

ire your decision: Be sure to tell your family...

SHARING YOUR DECISION to be an organ and tissue donor with your family is as important as making the decision itself. At the time of death, your family will be asked about donation. Sharing your decision with your family now will help them carry out your decision later. A simple family conversation will prevent confusion or uncertainty about your wishes. Knowing that they fulfilled your wish to save other lives can provide your family with great comfort in their time of grief.

It is also helpful to discuss your reasons for supporting donation with members of your family. Donor cards may also serve as a reminder to your family and medical staff of your personal decision to be a donor. Carry it in your wallet or purse at all times and encourage other members of your family to do the same.

If you would like to become an organ donor, you may register when you renew your driver's license. You might carry a note or card in your wallet, signed by two witnesses simply stating that, in the case of your death you would like your organs donated.

"For more information, please visit www.shareyourlife.org."

LAURA L. FINE

United Network for Organ Sharing

Patients Transplanted in the U.S.*
October 1, 1987-December 31, 2002
By Organ Received and Most Recent Status**

Organ	Number of Recipients (10/1/87 to 12/31/02)	Number of Recipients Reported with a Failed Graft but Not Reported Dead**	Number of Recipients Reported Dead**	Number of Recipients Not Reported Dead or with a Failed Graft**
Kidney	160,458	22,093	27,481	110,884
Kidney- Pancreas	10,524	2,231	1,856	6,437
Pancreas	2,880	655	423	1,802
Intestine	640	0	296	344
Liver	51,122	0	15,478	35,644
Heart	32,178	0	12,076	20,102
Lung	9,845	0	5,071	4,774
Heart-Lung	797	0	520	277
Total***	262,413	23,709	61,834	176,870

* The number of unique people who received each type of transplant between October 1, 1987 and December 31, 2002.

** The patient status is based on the most recent follow-up data received for each patient. A patient is known to be dead when a death follow-up is received. It is not known that all other patients are alive. This assumption could be false in cases where the patient is lost to follow-up, or the notification of death was not entered into the OPTN data before July 18th, 2003. Similarly, a kidney graft is known to have failed when a graft loss follow-up is received. However, it is not known that all other grafts are currently functioning.

*** The total does not equal the sum of all organs. This is due to those patients who received more than one type of organ transplant during the time period.

Based on OPTN data as of July 18th, 2003.
Data subject to change based on future data submission or correction.

End Notes

If you find yourself going through a spiritual crisis, health challenge, or emotional life struggle and are seeking ways to learn how to support these life changes I would like to recommend going spiritual shopping. This simply means taking some time to explore different spiritual paths or practices, anything that assists you in experiencing more love for God in your heart. If you would like further information about my personal spiritual practice you can find that easily on the website: www.BarsanaDham.org

For readers who wish to learn more about energy healing you may wish to refer to my web site: www.LionheartLA.com

I am co-founder of The Lionheart Institute of Transpersonal Energy Healing. Lionheart offers classes in Wholistic Healing through the development of spiritual qualities such as integrity, compassion, forgiveness, innocence, humility and love of self and others. Through

Laura (toward center) with students at Lionheart Central, San Antonio
Six months post transplant · 2001

the cultivation of these spiritual qualities we learn to responsibly practice the art of subtle healing for others. The focus is on our own healing. As a byproduct we achieve the art and skill of hands-on healing to assist others. The curriculum is grounded in the anatomical structure of the human physiology with special attention to practical medical application.

Lionheart Institute is structured primarily in a format of one-day and weekend long intensive trainings to accommodate participants from all over the country. Lionheart has three branches:

www.LionheartLA.com

www.LionheartTX.com

www.LionheartMidwest.com

These centers are located in Los Angeles, San Antonio and Milwaukee. Several times a year free introductory lectures and activities are available at each location. Please refer to the website for details.

LAURA L. FINE

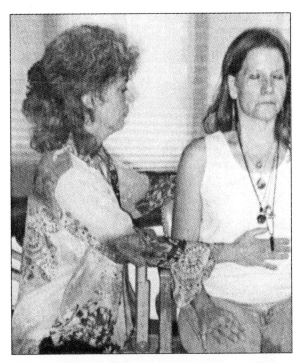

Laura demonstrating energy healing on a student
Eight months post-transplant · 2001

Laura Fine and Bunny Blair Rush, Co-Founders
Lionheart Institute of Transpersonal Energy Healing

LAURA'S NEW HEART — End Notes

About the Author

Laura has had a dual career in the creative and healing arts for twenty-five years. She holds two Masters degrees, one in Marriage and Family Therapy from San Diego University of Integrative Studies and a second Master's degree in Theatre Arts from the University of Miami, Florida. Through interweaving the creative and healing arts, Laura has recognized that "Healing is creating and creating is healing, and combing the two is fun!" She is committed to merging these realms when teaching her classes nationally and in her private practice in Los Angeles. She has been a licensed Holistic Health Practitioner and energy healer for twenty-five years having created and developed an acting technique called "The Energy System of Acting (ESA).

Laura worked professionally in the theater as a director and acting teacher for twenty years with numerous institutions including Manhattan Class company, Barnard College and Riverside Shakespeare Company in New York. Laura is also a graduate of the "Barbara Brennan School of Healing" and has extensively studied Kabbalistic Healing with The Society of Souls in New Jersey.

She is co-founder and Academic Director of "The Lionheart Institute of Transpersonal Energy Healing." The Institute has three national locations. They are located in San Antonio, Milwaukee and Los Angeles. Laura is currently implementing a pilot study in wholistic healing for heart transplant patients at U.C.L.A Hospital.

Having faced, survived and healed from a life-threatening illness, Laura recognizes the value of each moment of life and has great compassion for the struggles of the mind and heart.

Laura Fine helps us peek into the civil war created by heart failure. Through her struggles she matured and evolved as a person and shares with her readers a path to wellness that we can share.

Dr. Mehmet Oz, Heart Surgeon
author of *Healing from the Heart*
and host of television series "2nd Opinion with Dr. Oz"

Sometime in each physicians life a Laura Fine walks through the door. Focused on healing her heart through alternative medicine Laura forced me to make the decision of maintaining the physician-client relationship despite wanting approaches not consistent with medical doctrine. The result, a trusting relationship, a new heart and this wonderful book as a gift to heart patients all over the world.

Mimi Guarneri, M.D., F.A.C.C.
Medical Director, Founder
Scripps Center for Integrative Medicine

It was inspiring to be part of Laura's transition from an alternative healer to a heart patient, struggling with the ultimatum of transplant or death. In "Laura's New Heart" she gives her wisdom to those that are confronted with a similar dilemma. Laura's story is truly an integrative approach to healing blending the best of both worlds.

Rauni Prittinen King R.N., H.N.C, C.H.T.P./I
Manager, Founder
Scripps Center for Integrative Medicine

Laura Fine's book, "Laura's New Heart", is an wondrous account of a healer's journey to new life. It describes not only the "reality of our own mortality", but also reveals how through spiritual practice we can learn to become more reconciled with the pain of our own hearts. It shows us how to move beyond trauma and embrace life through an awareness of true being. This is a masterful healer's book, coming to us at a time when the world is desperately in need of healing.

Robin York
Ph.D. student, University of California, Santa Barbara

Printed in the United States
17414LVS00007B/100-168

9 781414 064338